T0194039

TOTAL RELAXATION

Also by Dr. Frederick Lenz

Lifetimes: True Accounts of Reincarnation

TOTAL RELAXATION

The Complete Program for Overcoming Stress, Tension, Worry, and Fatigue

by Dr. Frederick P. Lenz

The Bobbs-Merrill Company, Inc.
Indianapolis/New York

Copyright © 1980 by Frederick Lenz

All rights reserved, including the right of reproduction in whole or in part in any form
Published by the Bobbs-Merrill Company, Inc.
Indianapolis   New York

Designed by Sheila Lynch
Manufactured in the United States of America

10 9 8 7 6 5 4 3 2 1

Library of Congress Cataloging in Publication Data

Lenz, Frederick.
  Total relaxation.

  1.Relaxation. 2.Stress (Psychology) 3.Stress (Physiology) I.Title.
RA785.L46   613.7'0   79-55439
ISBN 978-1-9821-0230-2

*This book is dedicated
With Love And Gratitude
To Sri Chinmoy,
Who taught me that
The most beautiful flowers
Grow in the human heart.*

ACKNOWLEDGMENTS

We live in a world in which stress-causing factors are increasing at an alarming rate. But occasionally an individual emerges who has the inner fortitude, sensitivity, and positive energy to raise the consciousness of others. Sri Chinmoy is such an individual. I have had the opportunity of studying meditation with him for over ten years. A number of the approaches and techniques that are contained in the Total Relaxation Program have been adapted from his teachings. I would like to take this opportunity to thank him for his constant guidance, concern, and love.

I would also like to thank Phil Donahue and his producer, Pat McMillen, for their continuing contribution to American awareness. Unfortunately, television is one of the primary tension-causing factors in our contemporary lifestyles. But Mr. Donahue's program is an exception to the rule, and it is one of the few shows I strongly recommend to people who want to be relaxed, informed, and entertained.

Further thanks go to: Louis Simpson, Ph.D., poet, scholar, and perennial teacher. Often things he has said come back to me with renewed force.

Thanks also to:

Nina France, for her typing, suggestions, and happy thoughts.

Lynne Spaulding, my editor, for her erudite criticism and her own warmth and cheerfulness.

Jim Seligmann, my literary agent, who is not only a great agent, but a dear friend.

Jim Fisher, for his support and belief.

Marguerite Dwyer, for her gracious help.

And last, but not least, to my Father, whom I can never thank enough, and of whom I am extraordinarily proud.

Contents

Introduction

The single greatest killer in America today is stress. I am a physician. As I have worked in hospitals over the past years, I have noted an alarming increase in people suffering from stress-related problems. Some would say that our society has merely become more conscious of the effects of stress. But statistics, such as those quoted by Dr. Lenz, indicate otherwise. Hypertension, arteriosclerosis, and related diseases such as heart attacks, strokes, and kidney disease, affect millions of Americans each year. I have seen such results of stress in my patients and their families, my co-workers and my neighbors. Stress is not limited to those people seen in hospitals and doctors' offices. Every person every day must deal with stress. Your ability to respond to and withstand stressful situations will largely determine whether or not you will develop a heart attack or hypertension.

Much of what Dr. Lenz discusses in the first chapter may seem unpleasant, frightening, or irrelevant to your present state of health. However, it is important to realize that the early stages of these diseases may be difficult for you or your doctor to detect. I have seen many patients in intensive care units with their first heart attack, who say, "But Doc, I thought I was in perfect health. I have been working long hours with no difficulty and I've had no pains. How could I have a heart attack?"

We Americans are hard-working and hard-playing people. We seldom stop to examine ourselves when things seem to be going well. But, as Dr. Lenz suggests, the physical and emotional problems arising from stress, tension, and anxiety can develop very deceptively. We must examine every aspect of our lives if we wish to approach tomorrow without the crippling effects of a physical or emotional disability.

Doctors, psychologists, sociologists, and others have been aware of these problems for many years. Unfortunately, although we all saw the problem, none of us could find a prevention for the underlying disease: stress. Without a reliable and practical method to approach stress as a disease, most of us were helpless. Warnings are seldom effective unless an alternative lifestyle can be offered. We had no miracle medicines or operations for our patients. We were continually faced too late with the end result: a heart attack, stroke, or kidney failure.

For me, this has been an extremely frustrating situation. Ideally, a doctor should be an educator and advisor, helping each person to develop his own "health plan" to effectively prevent and solve his medical problems. For this to occur, both the physician and the patient must be interested in more than just treating the symptoms of disease.

Working with Dr. Lenz over the past few years has given me new hope for the future of medicine and health. In his book and seminars on Total Relaxation, he examines almost every possible stress-causing situation. It is the clearest, most comprehensive analysis I have found of stress and the related physical, emotional, and social problems.

The best part of this program begins where most previous books end, with the effective strategies and techniques for *overcoming* stress and tension. The strategies are practical, easily understood advice for restructuring living situations to reduce and possibly eliminate stress. The twelve relaxation techniques allow one to release tension and relax when stress cannot be avoided or prevented.

The combination of clear analysis of stressful situations, practical strategies, and effective relaxation techniques makes *Total Relaxation* the most useful and comprehensive guide available for understanding and combatting stress and its effects. When stress is responsible for approximately 50% of the deaths each year in our country, I feel that the necessity and worth of this book is inestimable.

May 27, 1979

DR. MARGARET GREENWALD
St. Vincent's Hospital and
Medical Center of New York

Preface:
How To Use This Book

The book that you are holding can change your life. If you follow the advice and strategies that are contained in it, and if you practice the Total Relaxation Core Techniques, you will be able to overcome stress, tension, worry, and fatigue.

We live in a world that is filled with stress. It is virtually impossible to escape from the causes of stress. Even if you were able to change your job, move to a new place, and make new friends, you would still be subject to the variety of stresses and tensions that have become part and parcel of our contemporary world. However, you no longer have to be the victim of dangerous environmental, psychological, and other stresses. You can overcome stress. By reading this book and employing the different aspects of the Total Relaxation Program you will be able to conquer stress for once and for all.

The Total Relaxation program is the most effective and comprehensive program ever devised to overcome stress. It has worked for thousands of others and it will work for you. The Total Relaxation Program has evolved over the period of the last ten years. During this time thousands of individuals have attended Relaxation Workshops that I have conducted throughout the United States, Canada, and Europe. It was in these seminars that the techniques and strategies which comprise the Total Relaxation Program were developed, refined, and tested. It was also during this time that the Total Relaxation tapes, visualization cards, and progress charts were developed.

While in the past I have presented parts of the Total Relaxation Program on radio and television shows, in my classes at The New School for Social Research, and in Total Relaxation Seminars, this book provides the first complete text of the Total Relaxation Program, along with the twelve incredibly effective Core Techniques.

The program has a twofold approach for conquering stress. At its center are the twelve Total Relaxation Core Techniques. One of these techniques is presented at the end of each chapter in this book. The second part of the program consists of strategies and approaches for overcoming stress, along with a brief explanation of what stress is and how it affects both your body and mind. I strongly recommend that you read the first chapter carefully—it contains information which is vital to your understanding of the consequences of stress, along with detailed instructions for the use of the Total Relaxation Core Techniques.

Life without Stress

After reading this book you will have a working knowledge of the entire Total Relaxation Program. By utilizing the different elements of the Program, you will be able to live a happier, healthier, stress-free life. Throughout the course of your life, you will encounter a variety of situations and circumstances which will place you under stress. At those times, if you refer back to this book, you will find strategies and exercises that will help you cope with and overcome these new sources of stress and tension. The following is a partial list of the most common causes of stress and tension which you may encounter in the coming years, and the chapters in which they are discussed.

Advertising, Chapters 2 & 4   Death, 3
Alcohol, 5   Diet, 5
Being Alone, 3   Divorce, 3
Business Readjustment, 4   Exercise, 6
Change in Lifestyle, 3   Failure, 2
Communication, 11   False Expectations, 2
Commuting, 4   Fear, 3

Some Final Thoughts

The Total Relaxation Program works. But YOU are the key element in the program. Unlike many other stress-reducing programs, which require a great deal of self-discipline, time, and effort, the Total Relaxation Program is both easy to use and highly effective. But even though this program has been specifically designed for busy, active people who do not have a great deal of spare time, it is still necessary for you to devote a few minutes of your time to it every day in order to make it work effectively. You will probably find that the time you devote to the Total Relaxation Program will be some of the most enjoyable moments of your day. Good luck!

Dr. Frederick P. Lenz
The New School for Social Research
July 7, 1979

One

Learning to Relax

∿

Insist on yourself; never imitate. Your own gift you can present every moment with the cumulative force of a whole life's cultivation; but of the adopted talent of another, you have only an extemporaneous, half possession.
                                            —RALPH WALDO EMERSON

Do you often feel tense or anxious? Do you have a quick temper that flares up unexpectedly, causing you to say unkind things to those you love? Do you have trouble falling asleep at night? After waking from sleep, do you still feel fatigued? Do you harbor feelings of resentment or frustration about your job, your family, your economic situation, or yourself? Do the muscles in your stomach or neck frequently become taut and strained? Are you under increasing pressure to do and produce more and more in less and less time? Are you receiving less satisfaction from your life than you feel you should be?

If your answer to any of these questions is yes, then rest assured that you are not unusual. Actually, it would be quite surprising if you didn't exhibit some of these "symptoms" of living in our twentieth-century global village.

Today we are facing an epidemic the size and consequences of which we have never known before—an epidemic of stress. All the plagues and widespread outbreaks of disease in man's history cannot equal this twentieth-century epidemic either in the number of fatalities it is causing, or in its emotional or economic costs. Stress is responsible for

1

over half the deaths in the United States and Canada every year. The chances are good that you have already contracted this deadly and crippling "disease," and unless you take immediate action to overcome it, you will succumb to its dire effects.

Do these statements shock you? They should, because they are true. If you are unable to overcome the devastating effects of stress on your mind and body, there is a strong chance that you will fall victim to a heart attack, stroke, hypertension, kidney disease, arteriosclerosis, ulcers, and a host of other psychological and nervous disorders.

In today's world it is virtually impossible to escape completely from stress; it is a component of our world. Your boss yells at you, your car breaks down on the way to an important meeting, your child is sick, you don't have enough money to pay your bills, the music your kids play is driving you up the wall—the list is endless. Every day you encounter thousands of tension-causing situations, each one of which is the cause of a potential heart attack or stroke.

You may think back fondly to the stories your grandparents told you about when, years ago, life was simpler and there was little stress and tension in daily life. But, for better or for worse, our way of life has changed, and, as a result, you are exposed to dangerous levels of stress every day.

The causes are so rooted in our contemporary lifestyles that it is unrealistic to think that they are going to disappear suddenly. On the contrary, it would appear that the amount of stress that you are being subjected to, like inflation, is rising at an alarming rate. The technological revolution of this century has completely changed our lifestyles, eating habits, types of employment, and other social phenomena. Most people find it difficult to cope with the constantly increasing pace.

At the same time, the overall quality of the food you eat and the air you breathe, combined with a lack of exercise, deprives your body of the resources it needs to adapt to the stringent demands of our world. The human body evolves at a gradual pace, and it has not yet had a chance to catch up with our new ways of living.

If you do not do something to alter your susceptibility to stress, you are running the risk of a complete physical or mental breakdown. You may be on the verge of such a breakdown right now, without realizing it. You have two clear-cut choices. You can either leave things as they are and subject yourself to the unspeakable consequences, or you can learn to relax.

The Nature and Causes of Stress

Stress is the internalization of an emotional conflict which occurs when you are not in harmony with a situation. Life is full of circumstances which will cause even the most cool and collected persons to become nervous and upset. When you react to a situation by feeling worry, anxiety, or tension, you are, in effect, creating your own internal conflict.

Both your hereditary and learned responses set off a biological trigger within your body every time you enter a stressful situation. This trigger, called the "fight or flight response," sets off a defensive chemical reaction within you which nature has designed to help you overcome stress. But if this biological trigger is continually activated by prolonged or repeated exposure to stress, it will result in the destruction, rather than the protection, of your body.

The fight or flight response was evolved after millions of years of evolutionary testing, and is exhibited by both man and animals. It provides a selective advantage for your survival by giving you a quick burst of strength and energy when you are confronted with something which threatens your well-being.

When you are subjected to a stimulus which causes you to feel stress, a complex chemical reaction takes place within your body. At that time, an area in your brain called the hypothalamus stimulates your sympathetic nervous system to secrete epinephrine, norepinephrine, and other hormones, all of which we commonly refer to as adrenalin. These chemical messengers enter your bloodstream and cause an immediate and dramatic rise in the rate of your heartbeat, blood pressure, respiration, and body metabolism. At the same time, your body directs more blood to your arms and legs, preparing you to either "fight" against and overcome the initial cause of your stress, or to take "flight" and escape it.

Throughout the course of man's history, the fight or flight syndrome helped ensure his survival by giving him the extra strength he needed in situations of crisis to overcome the cause of his stress. The primary causes of primitive man's stress were either direct physical confrontations with man or animal, or harmful climatic or environmental changes. In either of these two instances, an individual's survival would in some way be threatened and he would experience stress. This feeling would elicit his fight or flight response and place his body into high gear. His body would continue to give him the extra strength he required to combat the source of his stress until he overcame it, escaped, or died in the process of trying.

In most instances, the fight or flight response of early man would only have been triggered for a short time, after which his system would have returned to normal. The major exception to this would have been a dangerous and sustained change in his environment. If, for instance, he was exposed to extreme cold, his fight or flight response would continue to give his body extra strength to overcome the cold. But if he was unable to fight against the cold, or escape from it, he would eventually die from exhaustion and exposure.

The situation of a person living in the twentieth century, however, is far different from that of someone living even as recently as a few hundred years ago. Most persons find that they can neither effectively fight the cause of their stress, or run away from it. Contemporary life subjects you to continual stress. Since it is impossible to overcome or escape the causes of stress, your fight or flight response is continually elicited. In response to this, your sympathetic nervous system will continually pour adrenalin into your blood stream, causing a sustained rise in the rate of your heartbeat and the level of your blood pressure. This sustained increase in your blood pressure and metabolism will eventually damage your body.

Physical and Emotional Symptoms of Stress*

Often a person will not realize that he has been under a detrimental amount of stress until it is too late. The primary reason for this is that most individuals ignore their bodies' warning signals that mean they are being overtaxed by stress, believing that these "symptoms" of stress are either unavoidable or not important enough to warrant their attention.

The first step in overcoming stress is simply to be aware of it. The following are common symptoms of stress; they are your body's warning that it is being damaged. If you exhibit any of them, you are a victim of stress.

Typical Symptoms of Stress

1. A dry mouth.
2. A tendency to perspire.
3. A tense neck or back.
4. A nervous stomach or stomach cramps.
5. Aches and pains that do not have an organic cause.
6. Feelings of constant fatigue even after sleep.
7. Difficulty falling asleep or staying asleep.
8. Feelings of weakness.
9. Strained facial muscles or a nervous twitch.
10. A tremor or shaking in your hands.
11. Palpitations.
12. Rapid mood shifts.
13. Fears of being alone, with others, in new places, etc.
14. Irritability.
15. A quick temper.
16. Shortness of breath.

---

*It should be noted that some of the symptoms of stress can also be symptoms of other serious diseases. If you are in any doubt, consult your physician.

17. Chest pain or feelings of tightness in your chest.
18. Hypersensitivity or hyperactivity.
19. The inability to relax, and feelings of guilt when you do relax.
20. A constant craving for activity and stimulation.

The Consequences of Stress

It is currently estimated that over twenty-four million Americans suffer from hypertension (high blood pressure). High blood pressure is directly related to the amount of stress a person is subjected to. It is often referred to as the "silent killer" because it is a symptomless disease. Most individuals who have hypertension do not realize that they have the disease until it has developed to such a severe state that it is irreversible, or has caused other complications such as arteriosclerosis (hardening of the arteries).

Hypertension has been directly linked to heart disease, strokes, and kidney failure, the three diseases responsible for the majority of deaths in North America every year. Untreated hypertension will not go away by itself; in fact, it will eventually result in death.

In most cases, when individuals develop hypertension, their blood pressure will remain at a dangerously high level for the rest of their lives. But, owing to the development of several new drugs, the fatal effects of hypertension can be controlled to some extent. Use of these drugs, however, often is accompanied by unpleasant side effects ranging from nausea and dizziness to the loss of sexual potency. In addition, the victim of hypertension must see a doctor on a regular schedule and take the medications for hypertension every day *for the rest of his life*. Persons who have hypertension must also restrict their lifestyles and avoid overexcitement and unnecessary stimulation.

Who is Likely to Develop Hypertension?

Hypertension is a disease that affects persons in all age brackets and from all walks of life. Even children and infants can have high blood pressure. While it has been suggested that individuals whose parents have hypertension are more prone to the disease, it has not been conclusively established to what extent heredity contributes, if at all, to the development of hypertension.

Most people have a preconceived notion of what a person who develops hypertension is like. They assume that he or she is a compulsive achiever who is under constant pressure to succeed. But many people who appear to be calm and relaxed also suffer from hypertension. The only way to determine if you have the disease is to have your blood pressure taken.

Type "A" and "B" Personalities

Several psychological studies have suggested that persons with specific behavior patterns and personality characteristics are more likely to develop hypertension than individuals who do not exhibit the same behavior patterns and personality traits. Those more susceptible to high blood pressure have what is known as a "Type A" personality, while those less susceptible are said to have a "Type B" personality.

Dr. Meyer Friedman and Dr. H. Rosenman formulated the original classifications of the "Type A" and "B" personalities. Since their pioneering research, other studies have discovered additional behavior patterns and personality characteristics that suggest whether you have a "Type A" or "B" personality. The following list of questions has been made up from a compilation of these studies. By taking this quiz, you will be able to determine if you have a "Type A" personality. If you answer "yes" to *any* of the questions, then you fall into the "Type A" category and are considered to have a substantial chance of developing high blood pressure.

Type "A" Personality Quiz

1. Do you feel the need constantly to make others happy, even if making them happy means that you will be unhappy?
2. Do you usually talk, eat, or move quickly?
3. Do you find it difficult to listen to others when they are not discussing a subject that is of great interest to you?

4. Are you dissatisfied with all of your personal relationships?

5. Do you easily become impatient with others when they don't understand something as quickly or easily as you do? Do you find that you try to make them hurry because of your own impatience?

6. Do you feel that if you "let go" and just be yourself that members of the opposite sex will not be interested in you?

7. Do you feel that someone should always respect you if you respect him?

8. Do you feel that you must succeed at everything that you do, and if you fail to succeed at your job or in some other activity that there is something wrong with you?

9. Do you feel that spending too much time alone is not good for you?

10. When you are not working, or on vacation, do you have difficulty relaxing?

11. When you are trying to relax, or if you are not occupied in some specific task, do you feel guilty that you are not doing something?

12. Do you get angry easily?

13. Do you find that you can't talk easily to your friends and family, even though you want to?

14. Are you preoccupied with time and efficiency? Do you constantly feel that you have more and more to do in less and less time?

15. Do you feel the need to challenge others and compete with them?

Other Effects of High Blood Pressure

High blood pressure and stress are direct causes of many other diseases, the most important of which is arteriosclerosis. According to Dr. Herbert Benson, the Director of the Hypertension Section of Boston's Beth Israel Hospital, an individual's risk of developing arteriosclerosis (hardening of the arteries) is directly related to the level of his blood pressure. The rule of thumb is: the higher your blood pressure is, the greater your chances of developing arteriosclerosis. Arteriosclerosis causes your normally open arteries to become clogged with deposits of minerals and fats. As the disease progresses, the size of the passageway through which your blood flows becomes smaller and smaller. As your heart works harder to pump blood through partially clogged arteries, the muscle fibers within your heart increase and your heart grows larger. A heart that has increased in size requires more blood to feed its tissues. Thus a vicious cycle is set up. Your enlarged heart requires more blood and continually has to raise the level of your blood pressure to meet its ever-increasing demands. At the same time, your rising blood pressure escalates the development of arteriosclerosis, constantly making the passageway in your arteries smaller, which in turn requires your heart to work harder and enlarge even further. This cycle will normally end when several of your coronary arteries have become totally obstructed by the advancement of the arteriosclerosis, and a heart attack takes place.

One of the most famous studies of the devastating effects of hypertension on the body took place in Framingham, Massachusetts. The results showed that persons who have chronic high blood pressure have seven times as many strokes, three times as many heart attacks, and four times as much congestive heart failure as persons with normal blood pressure do.

Stroke

A cerebral hemorrhage, commonly known as a stroke, is often the devastating result of hypertension. Strokes are the third largest cause of death among people living in the United States. Most strokes occur in one of two ways: Either high blood pressure causes a blood vessel in the brain to burst or arteriosclerosis blocks the arteries within the brain, causing a blood clot to form. The results of stroke are temporary or permanent loss of memory and other functions of the intellect, partial or complete paralysis of the body, and in many cases immediate death.

Kidney Failure

High blood pressure often causes damage to an individual's kidneys. This usually occurs as arteriosclerosis blocks the renal arteries that supply the kidneys with blood. When this happens, the kidneys fail to function properly and are not able to remove the body's waste. In an attempt to remedy the situation, the kidneys secrete hormones that increase the blood pressure, further escalating the development of arteriosclerosis. This vicious cycle will only end when the arteries within the kidneys become so blocked that the kidneys completely fail.

Kidney failure can result in immediate or early death. The kidney patient must constantly undergo dialysis to remove the wastes from his system which his kidneys no longer filter. An individual who has lost the function of his kidneys will have to follow a restricted diet and drastically alter his lifestyle for the remainder of his life. In most cases, even with the aid of dialysis and kidney transplants, victims of kidney failure will lead much shorter lives.

Effects of Stress on the Mind

As we have seen, there is a direct connection between the amount of stress you are subjected to and the health of your physical body. But stress also has a dramatic effect on the functioning of your mind. While some individuals seem to be able to tolerate stress better than others, continual stress will eventually cause even the strongest persons to have a partial or complete mental breakdown.

Numerous studies have confirmed the detrimental effects of stress on the mind. A great deal of what we call mental illness has resulted from the inability of an individual to deal effectively with the pressures, demands, and stresses that modern life has placed upon him. Many of the less severe psychological problems develop because a person is simply unable to adapt to the changes and instability of our rapidly changing lifestyles. When a person feels that he can no longer cope with the stresses of his life, he will often retreat into himself and exhibit abnormal behavior patterns. Persons who suffer from stress are often subjected to unfounded attacks of anxiety, fear, insecurity, nervousness, and jealousy. Some persons exhibit very aggressive behavior and find themselves unconsciously taking out their frustration on their friends, families, employees, and co-workers. In almost all cases, persons who suffer minor psychological problems as a result of excessive stress find that they have a great deal of difficulty effectively communicating with others. This often increases their frustration and subjects them to even more of the damaging effects of stress.

Personality Immobilization

One of the commonest effects of psychological stress is personality immobilization. It surfaces in people's attitudes towards themselves, their job, their relatives and friends, and towards the structure and institutions of society. Personality immobilization prevents people from actualizing all of their innate capacities and talents. If it is untreated, it can often lead to more serious forms of mental illness. Many individuals who have been immobilized by stress are unaware of what has occurred to them. They have become so used to being immobilized that they no longer feel it is possible for them to change and overcome their limitations. If you answer any of the following questions affirmatively, you are experiencing some degree of personality immobilization:

1. Are you afraid of going new places or trying new things?
2. Do you feel that no one really loves or understands you?
3. Do you feel that you are not as good as everyone else is?
4. Do you feel that each time you overcome a problem or difficulty, another problem or difficulty is waiting to take its place?
5. Do you feel that you are sexually inadequate?
6. Do you feel the need to dominate others and always have them under your control?

7. Do you feel that your life is in a constant state of turmoil and that you never have even a moment's peace?

8. Are you constantly plagued by self-doubts, worries, and insecurities?

9. Do you avoid doing things you would like to do because you feel that doing things for yourself is selfish?

10. Do you feel guilty when you do things you enjoy doing?

11. Do you feel that the source of all of your problems can be traced to the government and the people who run it?

12. Do you feel that people in official positions, such as bankers, doctors, city officials, police officers, Internal Revenue Service workers, social workers, and others, are against you, or are trying to make things more difficult for you?

Neurosis and Psychosis

Continued exposure to high levels of stress can cause severe cases of mental illness. Manic depression, schizophrenia, paranoia, and many other mental disorders often have their roots in stress. When an individual is not able to deal effectively with stress, he may also turn to the use of hallucinogenic and narcotic drugs, the abuse of alcohol, cultism, and protracted flights of fantasy. Even after the original causes of a person's stress have been removed, he will often experience the negative aftereffects of these illnesses for many years.

The High Costs of Stress

Each year, the American public spends hundreds of millions of dollars to pay for their flirtation with stress. The following is a *conservative* estimate of some of the standard prices for treating diseases and ailments that are caused by exposure to stress. These estimates do not include calculations for the loss of a person's time when he is hospitalized or forced to stay away from work because of stress-induced illness. By the time you read this list, owing to inflation, these prices have already risen ten to twenty percent.

Hypertension

Initial visit to the Doctor	$50.00
Chest X-ray	25.00
Electrocardiogram	25.00
Blood tests	30.00
Medication	20.00
Total for the first visit only:	150.00

Subsequent visits and medication that will be
necessary each year for the rest of the patient's
life: 700.00

Heart Attack:

Intensive care unit,		
minimum 5 days @ $355.00 a day		$1,775.00
Each day in intensive care:		
Electrocardiogram	$25.00	
Chest X-ray	45.00	
Blood tests	30.00	
	100.00	
5 days total		500.00
Seven more days in		
regular hospital unit with tests		1,500.00
Home care, medications,		
additional doctor's visits, and tests		1,500.00
Total Cost for a Heart Attack		$5,275.00

Stroke:

Average cost: $5,000.00

Ulcers:

Including Doctor's office visits,
   stomach X-rays, and medication
   for treatment. Average: $350.00

While we can estimate the approximate cost of hospitalization for a heart attack or a stroke, the personal suffering and anguish that is brought about by ailments caused by stress cannot be estimated. How much is it worth to be constantly tension-ridden? What is the dollar compensation to your children if you die unnecessarily with a heart attack, stroke, or kidney disease? Is there any way to estimate the cost of the permanent loss of strength and physical health that occurs if you have a heart attack or stroke? What is the emotional cost of an unhappy life filled with constant disputes, arguments, and hostilities brought on by your exposure to stress? These are the hidden costs of stress which cannot be measured, nor will the victims of stress ever receive any compensation for them.

It's Up to You:
Total Relaxation and the Core Techniques

Until the early 1950's it was commonly believed that your ability to tolerate stress was hereditary. If, for example, your mother or father had high blood pressure, then it was assumed that you would have a high susceptibility to the same disease.

But the psychological studies of Dr. B. F. Skinner and other psychologists from the behaviorist school revealed that the majority of a person's actions and reactions are not the result of heredity, but of conditioning. Further, they discovered that it is possible to modify a person's learned behavior patterns through conditioning.

The discoveries of the behaviorists radically altered contemporary medical theories about stress. Since heredity was no longer considered to be the dominant factor in human behavior, it was accepted that man could consciously determine his own behavior patterns.

Viewed from this perspective, it became clear that a person's ability to withstand stress was a product of his education. Thus, if your mother or father was prone to nervousness or high blood pressure, it is unlikely that they passed their nervous temperament on to you in your genes and chromosomes. It is more likely that you exhibit a similar susceptibility to stress because you unconsciously modeled your behavior patterns on theirs.

When you were a child, if you observed your mother becoming upset and distressed after arguing with your father, then chances are you learned to respond to similar situations in the same way. As a result, whenever you have an argument with someone, you become upset because you are unconsciously imitating your mother's behavior.

The models on which you base your responses to stress, however, are not limited to your parents. Any person with whom you have come in contact, or read or heard about during your lifetime, may have served as one of your behavior models. If, for example, one of your elementary school teachers became upset when she was speaking to your class about a subject related to sex, then your own nervousness about sex may have been learned from her.

It is neither possible nor necessary for you to recall when and from whom you learned all your responses to stress. What is of paramount importance, however, is for you to realize that you have the power to redefine and change your reactions to stress. With proper guidance, you can unlearn your negative responses and learn new stress-free responses to situations and circumstances that formerly caused you to become upset and tense—and that is what the Total Relaxation Program is about.

The Total Relaxation Program teaches you how to relax by providing you with the most effective relaxation techniques known. It is a complete program consisting of two parts. First, there are twelve easy-to-use and effective core techniques that enable you to eliminate built-up stresses and tensions. By using the Total Relaxation Core Techniques, you will gain a new sense of mental clarity and peace. You will then be in a position to implement the second part of the program which consists of strategies for overcoming your negative reactions to very specific situations which may be causing you stress.

Using the Total Relaxation Core Techniques is both pleasant and easy. When you employ any of these techniques, you will spend a few minutes with your eyes closed visualizing or imagining pleasant scenes and images.

The visualizations used in the core techniques were not

randomly chosen. Through experimentation with a variety of archetypal image and symbol patterns I have been able to create twelve basic relaxation techniques that enable a person to enter quickly into a state of deep relaxation. Relaxation research has indicated that there are a number of sounds, images, and sound and image complexes which enable a person to enter into a state of deep relaxation. For example, many persons find it extremely easy to relax when they hear the sounds of ocean surf, rain, and "white noise." In my own research I have discovered that there are specific image and symbol patterns that work even more effectively than sound for inducing deep relaxation. These image and symbol patterns trigger psychological and subconscious relaxation responses. I have refined these techniques over the years and the result is the most effective group of relaxation methods available.

Total Relaxation is completely positive. There can be no negative results from practicing it. You can practice Total Relaxation at any time in any place. You can practice it every day, or only when you feel the need. Total Relaxation can be practiced either sitting down, standing up, or lying down. The position is not important. The recommended length of time for practicing Total Relaxation is from five minutes to half an hour. You can practice it for a shorter or longer period if you wish, without any adverse effects. During Total Relaxation, allow your breathing to seek its own level. It is usually desirable to have your eyes closed, but if you find it easier, leave them open.

You can practice Total Relaxation alone or with others. Whenever you find yourself becoming tense, irritable, worried, or in need of inspiration or rejuvenation, use one of the core techniques. They will work well at home, in your office or schoolroom, outdoors, or in virtually any surroundings. Try different Total Relaxation techniques. Eventually you will find one or more techniques that work best for you.

Use Total Relaxation whenever you feel tension. You will find that by taking a Total Relaxation break, you will be able to refresh and renew yourself and gain the energy and inspiration that will help you lead a happier and healthier life.

Using Total Relaxation Techniques

First read over the technique several times until you are comfortable with it and then try it. If worrisome thoughts pass through your mind during Total Relaxation, simply ignore them. It will only increase your tension to fight with your thoughts. If you have positive or creative thoughts during Total Relaxation, thoughts that make you happy or at ease, allow them to swim through your mind. They generate a positive mental energy that will help you relax. But when thoughts which make you tense, unhappy, or restless pass through your mind, simply choose to ignore them.

When you visualize the images used in the Total Relaxation techniques, it is not necessary to see a clear "picture" of them in your mind. If you cannot picture the images, simply think about them. When other images or pictures come into your mind, ignore them. The core techniques work well the first time you use them, and will work even more effectively with repeated use.

TOTAL RELAXATION TECHNIQUE #1
THE BLUE SKY

Picture a beautiful blue sky without any clouds in it. As you picture the clear blue sky, feel that your body is growing lighter and lighter. Close your eyes and keep the image of the blue sky in your mind. There are no limits to the blue sky. It stretches endlessly in every direction, never beginning and never ending. As you visualize the blue sky, feel that your body has become so light that you have floated up into the clear blue sky. Feel that you are floating in the sky and that all tension, fatigue, worry, and problems have left you. Relax your mind and allow your breathing to seek its own level. Feel yourself floating gently in the clear blue sky which stretches endlessly in every direction, never beginning and never ending.

After several minutes have passed and you feel yourself relaxing, then picture that your entire body is merging with the blue sky. Your body is merging with the peace of the blue sky ... Your mind is merging with the tranquility of the blue sky ... Feel that you have actually become the blue sky. You no longer have a body or a mind. You have become the infinite blue sky that stretches endlessly in every direction, never beginning and never ending. Feel that you have become the perfect peace and tranquility of the blue sky. Completely let go and experience Total Relaxation.

When you feel that you have relaxed for as long as you like, then open your eyes. You will now have a new and deeper sense of peace, relaxation, and poise. This renewed energy, joy, and calm will stay with you as you resume your normal activities.

Two

Overcoming
False Expectations

〜

> He who binds to himself a joy
> Does the winged life destroy
> But he who kisses the joy as it flies
> Lives in eternity's sunrise
> —WILLIAM BLAKE: "Eternity"

Stress is a learned response to specific circumstances. In order to eliminate stress you must first understand how you create it. Then, by employing the strategies that are contained in the following chapters, you will be able to conquer stress once and for all.

First, you need to give up blaming the world, society, your friends and relatives, your employer, your bad luck, your karma, your genetic make-up, God, life, or anyone or anything else for the way your life is. As long as you do that, you are relinquishing your power to change things, and it will be impossible for you to learn to relax. Once you accept responsibility for all of your actions, you empower yourself to determine new stress-free behavior patterns and stick to them.

Being responsible for yourself does not mean transferring *blame* to yourself, either. It is your acceptance of your own limitations, with a view towards transcending these limitations, that will enable you to understand and work with the total "you."

The Nature of False Expectations

Seen through your own eyes, you are a certain "type" of person who has a number of different strengths and weak-

nesses, likes and dislikes. You base your self-assessment on
your past performance. But if you believe that you are the
same as you were last year, last month, or even when you
started to read this page, then you are wrong. At every minute you are growing and changing. Your body is constructing
new cells, new thoughts and impressions are entering your
mind, and new possibilities and challenges are beckoning to
you. It's easy to fall into the trap of feeling that you are the
same. You have been "John Jones" or "Susan Miller" all of
your life. You have defined yourself. You feel that you have
certain talents and limitations. But all of these conceptions
are incorrect assessments of what you truly are. Although
you may have some temporary imperfections and limitations, inwardly you are as perfect as an unwritten number.

You are the end result of millions of years of evolution.
You are the best of Mother Nature's creations. You can do,
see, feel, and become infinitely more than you now are. But
you must first rid yourself of your limited way of looking at
yourself. Once you do this, you will automatically enter into
a natural state of relaxation and inner peace. But as long as
you allow incorrect ideas of yourself and false expectations
to dominate your life, you will not be able to overcome your
own limited self-image.

Most people find that it is impossible to relax because they
have been taught to expect too much from themselves. From
their earliest childhood they have been conditioned to expect
that they will perform in specific ways in a variety of situations. When you find yourself incapable of performing according to these expectations, or when you no longer want to
perform as you feel you are obligated to, you enter into a
state of inner conflict which eventually results in tension,
frustration, and depression. It is only by rëexamining your
priorities and reassessing your self-expectations that you
will be freed from these incorrect expectations and be able to
totally relax.

Expectation creates frustration. Whenever you expect
something from yourself or from anybody else, you are placing yourself in an emotionally vulnerable position and pav-

ing the way for tension. Consider your own life and the expectations that you have placed upon yourself in your daily routine. If you are single, you are expected to be actively enjoying yourself almost all of the time. You expect that you will be successful at your job, in your social relationships, and in all of the activities that you participate in. If you are married, you expect that you will be able to provide for your family, balance your budget, raise your children, get along with your relatives, and have a deep and meaningful relationship with your spouse. When you go on a vacation you expect that you will have "the time of your life" and that you will squeeze into one or two brief weeks all of the "fun" you didn't have all year long.

These and the other expectations you place upon yourself and your life can only lead to tension and frustration. You find that you are frustrated when you can't do everything you would like to and can't perform on the level at which you would like to perform. You also become tense and frustrated when things don't turn out as you had planned: when it rains on your vacation, when you can't afford to buy the things you would like to because of skyrocketing prices, when someone you love ignores you or is unkind to you. Yet you expect that you will be able to deal with everything in your life successfully. You have been conditioned to believe that you must succeed at everything you do regardless of how difficult or even how undesirable the things that you strive for may be. When you do succeed and everyone pats you on the back and commends your successful achievement, you swell with pride and feel happy with yourself. But this happiness doesn't last because you are expected to be more and more successful throughout your life. If you try to rebel against the success trap, you will find that pressure to conform will be exerted on you both from within yourself and by others.

The root of this problem is the equation that our society makes between happiness and success. If we trace our cultural heritage, it is easy to understand how this confusion of principles came about. Our Puritan forefathers believed that material success was a sign that God was pleased with them. When the neighbor's crops failed, or if several of his cows died, everyone in the community believed that it was because he had done something immoral or in some other way had displeased God. The average person today does not consciously feel that when he fails it is because he is sinful. But the cultural conditioning that he has received causes him to echo a thought that is probably not too different from the thoughts of one of his Puritan ancestors who had failed at something several hundred years earlier: "I failed because there is something wrong with me."

A familiar proverb tells us that: "To err is human, to forgive divine." We should change this maxim to: "To fail is human, to forgive our own failures is divine." When you fail at something and feel miserable, you are only limiting your own chances for future happiness. At the same time you are placing yourself in a state of tension and internal conflict.

Failure makes most people despondent. They lose their drive and vitality. They do more harm to themselves by brooding upon their failure than they would if they would accept their failure as a necessary part of the learning process and then forget it. After several attempts that end in "failure," most people give up. They feel that if they have failed before, they will probably fail again. If they would extricate themselves from the success trap, then they would not allow their so-called "failures" to upset them.

You must reeducate yourself to feel that there is nothing wrong with failure. In fact, failure is often a necessary step in achieving success. If you hadn't been willing to fall off your bicycle the first few times, you never would have learned to ride!

The motto of the General Electric Corporation is "Progress is our most important product." This is a good motto for each one of us. When we make progress at something, we feel inspired and we try to make even more progress. But you need to realize the difference between progress and success. Progress, in this sense, does not mean that we have succeeded. Success for most people means outlining a particular goal or plan and then fulfilling that goal or plan within a certain amount of time. Plans are a necessary and important part of living. But when you allow yourself to be dominated by your plans and goals, then you are losing the original purpose of your plan, which was to be happy. Lasting happiness comes from continual progress, and is not dependent upon achieving a particular goal.

If you want to escape the success trap, you must redefine success and failure: "Success is making progress. Failure is giving up."

Spontaneity and relaxation go hand in hand. When you are spontaneous, you are automatically in a relaxed state. Being spontaneous does not mean that you have to eliminate all planning and order from your life. On the contrary, being spontaneous means that you will allow yourself the option to change your mind when necessary. In order to be spontaneous, you must relax. If you are in a constant state of inner tension and turmoil, it is impossible to be spontaneous.

Being spontaneous means living each moment to the fullest extent. This particular moment will never come again. If you are tense and upset because your plans and expectations have not been fulfilled, you will miss the opportunities and joy that "now" offers to you. Your time is the most precious commodity that you have. Don't waste it.

A husband and wife who were in one of my classes at The New School related an experience of theirs to me that epitomizes this situation. Both of them work. Each year they take a vacation. They plan many activities that they feel they will enjoy. On their last vacation they decided to go to Florida. They spent several hours with their travel agent arranging all the details. When they flew to Florida for their vacation, they were very tired. Instead of relaxing for a day or two first, they were determined to use every possible moment of their two-week vacation for having "fun."

Their accommodations were not as nice as they had hoped they would be. They ate and drank to excess. During the last week of their stay the weather became unseasonably cold.

Instead of returning home, or taking the opportunity the cold weather provided to find indoor activities that they might enjoy, they continued to follow the plan of activities that they had outlined with their travel agent several months before. The end result of their vacation was that they returned home unhappy, exhausted, and overweight. As one of them remarked to me, "Some vacation, I was more tense trying to have a good time than if I had stayed on my job." They resolved not to go to Florida again, and to deal with another travel agent. At the time, however, they didn't realize that the reason they failed to return home relaxed and happy was that they had worked too hard at having fun. They were so determined to succeed at having "fun" and "relaxing" on their vacation that they did not deviate from their original plan which had been conceived months before when they were in an entirely different state of mind. If they had allowed themselves the freedom to depart from their original plan, they would have had a good time despite the bad weather and poor hotel accommodations.

One of the secrets of relaxation is enjoying the passage of time. In order to have the time of your life, you have to enjoy the time in your life. Don't fool yourself into thinking that fulfilling all your plans will make you happy. This will only increase your tension now and your frustration later. Simply allow yourself to enjoy the variety of experiences that life presents to you. If you are miserable being a student and you feel that being the teacher will change that, then you are wrong. Relax now and appreciate this particular moment in your life.

In order to be relaxed, you must choose to relax. Naturally, we assume that everyone wants to be relaxed and have inner peace. But to judge from the actions and behavior of most persons, it would appear that they deliberately place themselves in situations that make them tense. Most people find it difficult to relax because they have made choices they felt they *should* have made, instead of choices they wanted to make. If you answer any of the following questions affirmatively, then you fall into the category of persons who make choices not because they want to, but because they have been conditioned by their relatives, friends, and society to expect that these are the choices they should make.

1. Do you buy clothes that others will like, or do you buy clothing that only appeals to you?

2. Do you feel the need to be popular and well-liked?

3. Do you feel that you should listen to the advice of your family before making an important decision?

4. Do you feel that if you do not succeed at your job and continue to advance, something is wrong with you?

5. Do you feel the constant need to make others happy, even if it means that you will be unhappy?

6. Do you feel that spending too much time alone is not good for you?

7. Do you feel that someone should respect you if you respect him?

8. When you buy a car, are you more concerned about how it looks, or about the car's performance?

9. Do you feel that if you "let go" and just be yourself, members of the opposite sex will not be as interested in you?

10. Do you regret not taking opportunities that were offered to you in the past?

11. Are you dissatisfied with your current employment?

12. Are you dissatisfied with the personal relationships you have?

While the preceding questions do not take into account all of the possibilities that affect self-expectation, by taking this sample quiz you will be able to determine whether your expectations of your own behavior are self-motivated or whether you have been unduly influenced by others. Chances are that the choices you make are not motivated by your own desires, but by the desires and expectations that you have been taught to have. As long as you continue to have these false expectations of yourself, you will remain dissatisfied with your life. Even if you manage to fulfill all of your expectations, you will discover that these were not the things that you truly wanted. If you are unable to fulfill all of your expectations, you will feel that you have failed yourself and others.

One of the maxims of the advertising business is: Create a need, satisfy that need, and perpetuate it. One of the goals of advertising is to make you feel that you need things which you really don't need and to get you to spend money that you don't have on them. This same principle is probably at work in your life now. You have been taught that you need many things which you don't need at all. If you don't fulfill those needs as most "normal people" do, you are taught to feel that there is something wrong with you. But once you have fulfilled your so-called "need," you have to continue to want or need that thing which you didn't really want in the first place. If you try to reject these expectations which are placed upon you, you will be alienated from the so-called "happy people" who are having a wonderful time busily fulfilling needs that really don't exist. These are those smiling people that we see in television commercials who seem to find total fulfillment by using a new dishwashing liquid or by buying the latest model car.

The case of a young woman named Mary will illustrate this phenomenon. When I met Mary, she had just left her second husband. She was in a complete state of inner tension. She had been to a psychiatrist who had given her large quantities of Librium and other tranquilizers. But she wanted to be able to eliminate her tensions without drugs. She realized that taking "tranquilizing" drugs was not treating her problem, but only her symptoms. As soon as she stopped taking the tranquilizers, she was the same tense and nervous person that she had been before.

Mary had grown up in a small city in Connecticut. She had been told by her mother and other relatives that one of the most important things in life was catching a man who would be a good provider. Her mother had assured her that happiness came from having a good marriage and lots of children. She assumed that her mother was right. She devoted most of her adolescent years to trying to find the right man to marry.

She spent hours on her makeup, hair, and clothes. When she was twenty, she met a young man who proposed to her. When she told her mother about her possible marriage, her mother burst into tears, hugged her, and then immediately began to think of who to invite. Mary became so carried away with the preparations for the wedding that she ignored the part of herself that kept telling her that this young man was not the man she had wanted to stay with for the rest of her life. Even on the day of her wedding, when she suddenly got "cold feet" and thought that she should postpone her wedding, she got herself to go through with it because all the preparations had already been made. She thought of how embarrassed she and her mother would be if she cancelled the wedding on the day of the ceremony, so she married someone she really didn't want to.

The marriage was not successful. Mary and her husband weren't suited for each other. But Mary had always been taught that divorce was wrong, so she was determined to stick it out. She accepted her unhappiness as a temporary stage in her marriage and thought that it would pass as time went on. But instead of ending, her unhappiness only increased. After her second year of marriage, her mother and other married friends started to ask her when she was going to have children. Mary and her husband wanted to have children, but had not been able to. Naturally, Mary blamed herself. She assumed that there was something wrong with her. She had been taught that all normal girls grow up, get married, have children, and are happy. She had at least managed to get herself married, but she felt that even that was a failure because she couldn't seem to make it work.

Mary eventually became so tense and overwrought that her husband divorced her. She moved back in with her parents because she was afraid to be alone. Instead of enjoying her new-found freedom, she decided that the best thing she could do would be to remarry as soon as possible, feeling that this time she would "make it work." Her second marriage was even worse than her first. But this time she managed to muster up the courage to leave her husband before he left her. Her sense of self-defeat and failure were overwhelming. She had convinced herself that everything that had gone wrong with both of her marriages had been her fault. She now believed that she was incapable of doing anything right.

The world is filled with people like Mary. They have been taught to have expectations which are impossible to fulfill. They blame themselves and become tense and worried when they fail to achieve goals which were given to them by others. Instead of learning from their mistakes to reëvaluate their choices, they try and make up for their failures by responding with the same kind of negative behavior and choice patterns that caused their initial problems. This is the same logic that is used by the compulsive gambler who feels that he will make up for all of his losses by betting more money on "the next one." He does not realize that he should either accept that losing is part of the game, or give up gambling.

Overcoming False Expectations

In order to overcome your false expectations, you must first determine what your expectations are, and whether you have chosen them for yourself or if you have unconsciously let others "choose" them for you. The easiest way to do this is to make a list of all of your major expectations for yourself and then make a second list of your expectations for your family and friends. A typical list will look something like this:

My Expectations

1. I expect that I will succeed at my job.
2. I expect that I will earn more money next year.
3. I expect that I will fall in love with someone new.
4. I expect that I will make my family happy.
5. I expect that I will succeed at whatever I do.
6. I expect that I will not be lazy.
7. I expect that my friends and family will not let me down.

8. I expect that my partner will love me as much as I love her (him).

9. I expect that my children will respect me.

10. I expect that I will be happy if I can get all of the things that I want in life.

11. I expect that I will be happy if someone truly loves me.

12. I expect that I will always be attractive and will perform well sexually.

13. I expect that my plans for my life and the lives of my children will work out.

The list will be different for each person. But by making a list of your expectations and evaluating them, you will be able to determine which of those expectations are really valuable, and whether you have a good chance of fulfilling them or not. After you have completed this process, write down on a separate sheet of paper the following statement.

My Expectations

I have only one expectation, and that is that I will be myself in all situations and circumstances and that I will always be honest and true to myself. I do not expect that I will be able to do this right away. I will continue to try to make progress and I will be satisfied with myself, not because I have achieved this goal or failed, but because I am trying.

Using the "Now" to Defeat False Expectations

The future is now. The past is dust. Your acceptance of these two seemingly simple statements will do more to help you overcome your negative expectations than almost anything else. Both of these statements are declarations of independence for you in your war against stress and tension.

The future is now. This relatively innocuous statement demands your attention. It wants you to change the way you live. Instead of always living for the future, always expecting that *tomorrow* will bring you happiness, fulfillment, and success, you must come to realize that the future will not do or bring you anything. The future doesn't even exist. How can you hope to expect something from a non-existent reality? Yet every day you think in terms of the future. You are constantly planning, hoping, and expecting. But, for a moment, think back upon all of the expectations for the future you have had throughout the course of your life. How many of those expectations have turned out the way you thought they would? If you are like most people, then chances are that few, if any, of your expectations have come true. Did you, ten years ago, expect to be as you are now? Was there any possible way you could have foreseen the turns your life has taken? What good did all of those expectations do you? The only result of your expectations was worry, tension, and frustration. Your expectations did not alter the future in any way. They only succeeded in putting your own happiness and fulfillment a little farther out of reach.

The past is dust. Another innocuous-looking statement. But your understanding and acceptance of these four words can change your life forever. If you can allow them to enter into your consciousness and work for you, then you can do, be, and achieve much more than you ever thought you were capable of.

Consider the past. Can you see, feel, or touch it? Can you give it to someone else? Can you use it to pay your mortgage or rent? Is it really all that valuable? But you cling to it as if it was the most precious thing in your life. You identify with your past successes and failures, believing that what you are today is determined by what you were yesterday. You limit yourself by choosing to think about something that no longer exists. Your considerations of the past, like your thoughts of the future, only hold you back and place you in an emotionally vulnerable position.

False expectations always occur in either a non-existent future or past. If you can understand the essential fallacy in this type of thinking, then it will be easier for you to eliminate it from your life. By accepting that only "now" exists, that the future exists only in your imagination, and the past in your memory, you will be able to parry the devastating blows of your negative expectations.

The essential point is this: It is necessary for you to stop living your life in abstract time. The only time that exists is now. Stress and tension are products of your reliance on a non-existent future and past. Your conceptions of the past and future are the framework on which you build your false expectations. The easiest way to defeat your false expectations is to live in the now. Now!

Strategies for Eliminating False Expectations

● Begin your campaign to eliminate false expectations by recognizing them as sources only of anxiety and worry. Nothing constructive will come from your expectations. They will only alienate you from your real potential.

● Always postpone all important decisions to the last possible moment. When you make decisions too far in advance, you prevent yourself from being spontaneous. You also prevent yourself from utilizing new data and understandings to influence your decisions.

● Try to imagine yourself without any expectations. Imagination is an important first step in changing yourself. If you can imagine yourself being free from expectation and living only in the "now," then it will be much easier for you to effect this new perspective on your life.

● Do not be afraid of "failure." If you expect you must succeed at everything you do, you are only allowing the expectations of others to influence you. Remember that failure is just an arbitrary definition of a particular set of circumstances. There is only one type of failure, and that is when you give up. As long as you continue to try, you will make progress, and remember that progress, however slow it may be, is the real success.

● Do not attempt to rid yourself at once of all the false expectations you have built up over the years. If you "expect" to overcome all of your false expectations right away, you are only falling into the expectation trap again. Simply by becoming aware of your expectations, you will have taken the first step. Then gradually, one by one, consider your expectations. Realize that each expectation will only lead you to frustration. The gradual approach is the best method when dealing with expectations.

● Give up your old thoughts about the way you were. When you cling to what you used to be yesterday, you severely limit what you are today. Your ideas about the way you were in the past only immobilize you. Yesterday did not give you everything you wanted. If it had, you would have been totally satisfied. In the same sense, the way you were in the past was fine for the past, but today you want to grow beyond your limitations, tensions, and frustrations. The best way to do this is to feel that "the past is dust." Leave it behind you. Enjoy the now. Remember that this particular moment will never come again. Ride this moment and it will take you towards fulfillment.

● Make a list of all your expectations. Look at them and realize that none of them are going to help you in any way. They are simply projections of your worries and insecurities. The best attitude towards the future is this: If you can do, be, and become all you are capable of now, then the future will take care of itself. Have more faith in yourself and the process of life. Life has brought you this far, it's not going to let you down now.

● Make it a point not to expect anything from others. Whenever you expect something from someone else, you place yourself in an emotionally vulnerable position, and you place unfair limitations upon the other person. Enjoy people the way they are. Don't try to change them to suit yourself. You will discover that when you don't make demands and expect things from others, people will appreciate you and be drawn to you because they recognize that you like them for what they are. Do you like it when someone expects things of you? Don't expect anything from others, and you will never be frustrated by them.

● Don't expect anything from life. Do your best at whatever you do, but don't expect rewards. The most important reward that you can get is the reward of having a relaxed, happy, and full life. Do you really think that a "gold watch" will compensate you for a lifetime? Have the time of your life by enjoying the time in your life. Don't think about future rewards. Remember, if you are not happy with the way your life is now, you probably won't feel any different if the circumstances of your life change tomorrow. The key to overcoming stress is being happy. But happiness has little or nothing to do with your circumstances in life. Happiness is a result of your acceptance of yourself and life the way it is, without expectations. Once you have accepted yourself without placing any particular expectations on yourself, you can begin to transform yourself to be more of what you would like to be.

● Whenever you find yourself thinking about your future expectations, mentally repeat "The future is now." Whenever you think about the past, mentally repeat "The past is dust." By doing this *every time* you think of the past, or of your future expectations, you will train yourself to focus exclusively on the present moment.

● Try and keep your plans flexible. Avoid unnecessary planning. Try to make the necessary arrangements for your future without coupling them with expectations. If your plans go awry, don't become frustrated. Accept what happens as an opportunity to have a new type of experience. Instead of complaining, get busy at enjoying.

● Don't be limited by your plans or by the opinions of others. Don't be afraid to say "I don't" on your wedding day, or to change your mind at any time or at any important moment. You alone will have to live with your decisions, no one else. If you try to live your life to fulfill the expectations of others, then you will lose your self-respect. Be true to yourself.

TOTAL RELAXATION TECHNIQUE #2
THE TOWER OF LIGHT

Take a deep breath and exhale slowly. As you exhale, mentally picture all tiredness, tension, and fatigue leaving you. Relax. Turn your attention to the crown of your head. Visualize that a wave of golden light is entering into you at the top of your head and passing throughout your entire body. Imagine this golden light passing from the crown of your head, through your neck, shoulders, arms, chest, stomach, lower back, and down your legs to your feet.

As you imagine the golden light passing throughout your body, feel yourself relaxing. Picture another wave of golden light entering in through the crown of your head and visualize it passing through your entire body and then leaving through the soles of your feet. Feel that wave after wave of golden light is passing through you in this way. Each wave of golden light that passes through your body removes more of your tension and helps you to enter further and deeper into a state of total relaxation.

Picture that the waves of golden light have now become a solid river of golden light which is constantly passing through you. Picture this golden light expanding beyond your body and filling up the entire room. Then visualize the golden light expanding beyond the earth ... beyond the sky ... into the infinite. Feel that the golden light is constantly passing through you and washing all of your tensions, problems, and worries beyond you, beyond the earth ... beyond the sky ... into the infinite. Continue visualizing the golden stream of light passing through you into the infinite for as long as you choose to relax.

Three

Overcoming Psychological Stress

I believe that men are generally still a little afraid of the dark, though the witches are all hung, and Christianity and candles have been introduced.

—HENRY DAVID THOREAU: *Walden*

Psychological stress is the result of unresolved conflicts within your mind. These conflicts occur when you are flooded with negative thoughts and emotions. This is probably the most difficult type of stress to overcome because it is part of your psychological make-up. But by following the strategies outlined in this chapter, and by *repeatedly* applying them to the causes of your psychological stress, you will be able to eliminate the negative thoughts that deprive you of inner peace.

Worry, fear, and doubt are the major causes of psychological stress. Just one small fear, doubt, or worry can destroy your inner peace and place you in a potentially dangerous state of tension. If you do not consciously reject a negative thought, then other negative thoughts will quickly follow in its wake. The cumulative effect of negative thoughts is to immobilize you and prevent you from making correct choices and decisions. Once you have been overwhelmed by negative thoughts, it is difficult to recall what the original cause of your stress was.

Fears, self-doubts, worries, and other negative thoughts never produce any beneficial results. They don't help you to overcome any obstacles or succeed at any endeavors. They

35

only bring you down and rob you of your health and happiness.

Worry, A Self-Defeating Activity

Throughout your life you have had many occasions to worry. You have probably spent many hours worrying about whether you were going to succeed, worrying about your health, worrying about the health of your family and friends, worrying about money, worrying about death, worrying about your relationships with others, and so on. Now ask yourself, have your worries ever changed the final outcome of any of these situations? The answer of course is no. Your worries never improve the outcome of any situation. All they do is to place you under stress and drain your energy. Your worries can even negatively affect a situation. If you waste a great deal of your energy in worry, you will not be able to perform as well. If you are running in a race and you are constantly worried about how you are going to do or whether or not someone is about to pass you, you will not run as well. The reason for this is that you expended part of the energy you could have used for winning the race, in worry. If you had not allowed yourself to worry, and instead had directed all of your energy towards winning, you would have run a better race.

Worry is a type of self-defeating behavior with no positive benefits at all. Fear and doubt are two similar forms of unnecessary self-defeating behavior which place you under dangerously high levels of stress.

You must consciously decide to reject your negative thoughts. It is only through your conscious effort that you will be able to eliminate them from your life. The best remedy for your negative thoughts is to foster the growth of positive ideas and ideals within your consciousness.

Fear: The Pointless Emotion

Probably the single greatest cause of psychological stress is fear. Whenever you are afraid, you experience tension and anxiety, and enter into a state of mental paralysis that prevents you from marshalling your energies to overcome the causes of your fear. Fear will never help you deal with or overcome any difficulty you may face. On the contrary, fear drains your energy, places you under a burden of tremendous stress, and prevents you from acting with calmness and clarity. When you are paralyzed with fear, you are an easy victim for other fears and negative emotions. The only way to rid yourself of fear is by consciously rejecting it. First, you must learn to detach yourself from the cause of your fear. Second, understand that your fear is groundless, and finally, act with courage.

The Problem-Solving Formula

When you are attacked by fear, often you are so overwhelmed that you are literally swept away by the state of panic your fear creates. At such times, in spite of your best intentions, you lose control of your emotions. No matter how many resolutions you have made, fear and other negative emotions will overwhelm you until you have devised an effective formula for overcoming your difficulties. What can you do when fear and other negative emotions strike? Try the following formula:

Be Still — Evaluate — Then Act With Courage

Be Still

When fear strikes, it is important that you act immediately. The longer you delay, the stronger your fear will become, and consequently the more difficult your fear will be to overcome. As your fear grows in intensity, there will also be a parallel rise in your blood pressure, heart rate, and body metabolism. Fear will continually elicit your fight or flight response, creating dangerously high levels of stress. When you feel the first wave of fear beginning, employ the first part of the fear formula: Be Still. You must slow your-self down and not let your fear carry you away. You can stop any fear or negative thought in its tracks by using an affirmation.

An affirmation is a highly charged positive thought which enables you to bring yourself into a higher and more positive state of consciousness. An affirmation literally forces any negative thought or emotion out of your mind by virtue of its own strength. It is impossible for light and dark to exist in the same place. If a room is dark, and you switch on the lights, then darkness leaves the room immediately. In the same sense, it is impossible for you to have both positive and negative thoughts in your mind at the same time. If you can bring positive thoughts into your consciousness, then negative and destructive thoughts and emotions will leave you of their own accord.

Positive thoughts have a power all their own. Your positive thoughts enable you to actualize your full potential. They are the foundation of a new and better you. When you use an affirmation, you are consciously rejecting your negative thoughts and using your stronger positive thoughts to replace them. So allow your positive thoughts to help you defeat your worries, fears, doubts, and other problems.

There is no best affirmation. You can use one of the following affirmations or make up one of your own. It is generally a good idea in the beginning to write your affirmation down on a piece of paper and carry it in your wallet, purse, or somewhere on your person. If you are overcome by fear or any other useless emotion, simply read over your affirmation several times and continue repeating it over and over until your negative thoughts and emotions have disappeared. You can be involved in any physical action while you use your affirmation. Just repeat the affirmation silently within your mind. Don't give up! Sometimes it may take ten or fifteen minutes to overcome very powerful attacks of fear, doubt, and depression. You will find that the affirmation will work more powerfully with repeated use. It is an extremely effective strategy for raising the level of your consciousness.

Sample Affirmations

1. I am a good and worthwhile person with an inexhaustible capacity for happiness.

2. I am a good person who has a great deal to offer to others.

3. Inwardly I am as perfect as an unwritten number.

4. I am not my problems or limitations. I am a free spirit that flies through the skies of happiness.

5. I have no limitations except those I choose to place upon myself.

6. My real name is happiness.

7. I have come from delight, I exist in delight, and I will eventually become delight.

If, in the beginning, you fail to use an affirmation when fear or doubt overtakes you, don't be discouraged. Learning to use an affirmation is similar to learning to change the way you pronouce a word. When someone tells you that you have been mispronouncing a word, you will probably not correct yourself immediately. The first time that you say the word after you have been corrected, you will still say it incorrectly. You will realize your mistake a moment after you have made it. The next time you say the word, you will catch yourself halfway through your mistake, and then correct it. But the third or fourth time, you will correct yourself before you make the mistake. After preventing yourself from mispronouncing the word several times, the process becomes automatic and you no longer mispronounce the word.

Learning to use an affirmation is a similar process. If you don't use it immediately and your anger or fear gets the best of you, don't be upset. Next time you will use it sooner. Eventually, you will learn to stop your fears and other negative emotions before they start. Use of your own statement of affirmation will prevent you from entering into a tense and nervous state and you will be able to remain cool, calm, and relaxed.

Evaluate

The second step in the Problem-Solving Formula is to evaluate. Once you have detached yourself from your fears (or other negative emotions), you will be able to evaluate them and realize that they are totally useless emotions. By evaluating your fears you will be able to neutralize their effect upon you.

Consider how senseless your fear is. Realize that your fear will not help you deal with the problem or obstacle that is causing you to become afraid. Use the strategies in the remainder of this chapter to evaluate and defeat your fears and other negative emotions. Remember, your negative emotions will not help you to overcome your difficulties. They will only cloud the real issues by confusing you and draining you of the energy you need to overcome your difficulties.

Acting With Courage

After you have evaluated your fear, employ the last part of the formula: "Act With Courage." Acting with courage enables you to face your problem squarely. Running away from the causes of your worries and tensions only makes matters worse. Facing up to your problems with a cheerful and courageous attitude will enable you to defeat them.

You have an inexhaustible supply of courage within you. If you do not consider yourself to be a courageous person, then you have incorrectly assessed yourself. The difference between a hero and a coward is that the hero accepts his courage and uses it. A hero doesn't have any more courage than anyone else. Whether you consider yourself to be an essentially courageous person or not is irrelevant. Remember that the past is dust. How you acted or what you said yesterday does not have a direct bearing on what you are today. If you accept that you have an inexhaustible supply of courage, and you realize that acting with courage will enable you to defeat your destructive thoughts and emotions, then you can solve even the greatest problems. Remember, courage is not something you have to acquire. You already have it. You simply have to use it when the necessity arises. Life is not for the weakling; it is for the strong. You are strong. But you must consciously draw upon your inner strength to meet the challenges of your existence.

Making a "Fear List"

Making a list of your principal fears will help you to understand and defeat them. List, in order of importance, all of your major fears on a piece of paper. Your fear list may include some of the following fears.

Sample Fear List

1. I am afraid of dying.
2. I am afraid of meeting new people.
3. I am afraid of going to unfamiliar places alone.
4. I am afraid of the dark.
5. I am afraid of living alone.
6. I am afraid of leaving my job for another job.
7. I am afraid of pain.
8. I am afraid of moving to a new state.
9. I am afraid to tell others what I really think.
10. I am afraid of what I really am.
11. I am afraid of being separated from the people I love.
12. I am afraid of fear.
13. I am afraid of leaving my marriage and trying to make it on my own.

After you have made a list of your principle fears, then classify them according to their type. Doing this in advance will help you defeat your fears later when they strike you unexpectedly. The five principle classifications into which most fears fall are: (1) fear of the unknown; (2) fear of change; (3) fear of pain; (4) fear of yourself; and (5) fear of fear. Take each one of your fears and assign it to one of these categories. Then, after carefully reading over the following strategies for defeating these types of fears, apply these strategies to your own particular fears. By doing this you will easily be able to defeat even the strongest of your fears.

Fear of the Unknown

Once upon a time, a group of blind men were walking down a street. One of the blind men stumbled and fell over what he thought was a snake. He yelled in terror to the other blind men, "Save me, there's a snake here! Help!" The other blind men came over and started hitting the snake with their canes, and in doing so, accidentally struck and hurt the fallen blind man. Fortunately, another man who wasn't blind came along at that moment and saw the blind men were hitting a big coil of rope. He told them of their mistake and they all sighed with relief. But unfortunately, in his haste to escape the "snake," the first blind man had broken his arm.

Are you like the first blind man, trying to escape from something you can't see, but that you suppose will harm you? Are you still afraid of the dark, and all of the other fears you have accumulated over the years? Try this experiment. Go into a dark room and sit for a few minutes. Allow your imagination to create a phantasmagoria of horrible monsters that are waiting in the room to get you. Then, when you are sufficiently frightened, turn on the lights. The result? There was nothing to be afraid of all along. You simply created your own fears out of the flux of your imagination. This is true of all fears. Use the Problem-Solving Formula to eliminate your fears and act with courage. You are the source of all your fears and you can end them all. Do it! Now!

When you think of the unknown, what images come to your mind? Do you connect the unknown with danger and feelings of uneasiness? If you are like most people, you probably feel that the unknown is unsafe. Whereas you feel that circumstances, places, and people you already know are safe. But your fear of the unknown prevents you from going new places, meeting new people, and pursuing other activites that would improve the quality of your life. You fear the unknown because you have been taught to make the following equations:

$$\frac{\text{The Known}}{\text{Safety and Security}} = \text{Happiness}$$

$$\frac{\text{The Unknown}}{\text{Danger and Insecurity}} = \text{Unhappiness}$$

These equations, which have been fostered by our parents, friends, teachers, and the institutions of our society, are based upon two false premises. The first false premise is that it is possible to stay with the known and avoid change. The second false premise is that the known brings happiness and the unknown brings unhappiness.

The idea that you can escape from the unknown, or that it is even desirable to do so, is absurd. How can you escape from change? You can't. Everything that exists is constantly changing and becoming new and different. You yourself are new at every moment. This particular second has never existed before. How can it possibly be part of the known?

Fear of the unknown attacks you because you have accepted the idea that those things and situations with which you are unfamiliar are potentially harmful. For this reason you will avoid going to new places, meeting new people, eating out in new restaurants, changing jobs, moving to a new house or apartment, wearing a new hairstyle, implementing new business procedures, or making new investments. While it is certainly not desirable to leap before you look, this overcautious approach to life stifles your own growth, happiness, and productivity. Think back on the events of your life. When you have entered into new situations, traveled to unfamiliar places, or met new people, has it helped or hurt you? The new avenues that change has opened for you have added to, not detracted from, your life. Your continued association with the familiar things in your life will not promote any positive changes in your life. If you always stay with what is familiar, your life will be extremely boring, and you will be making another equation:

$$\frac{\text{The Known}}{\text{No Change}} = \text{No Growth}.$$

If you stay with that which is familiar, then you will stay as you are now, with all of your limitations, problems, and difficulties. Everything you know has not helped you overcome your imperfections. If it had, you would be perfect already. So it is only logical to assume that if what you know (the known) has not brought you everything you want and need, then in order to get it, you must enter into the unknown.

Fortunately, life does not permit you to stay with the known. At every moment you are hurtling through time and space into the unknown. But you can limit your entrance into the unknown, and in so doing, limit your growth. Your desire to stay with the known is predicated upon the idea that the known is safe and that the unknown is unsafe. But this is simply not true. Exploring the unknown does not mean opening yourself up to unpleasant or harmful experiences. You must learn to have faith in the process of life. Your belief that the known is safe is wrong. Consider another equation:

$$\frac{\text{The Known}}{\text{Safety}} = \text{Stagnation.}$$

You can die of as many diseases at home as you can anywhere else. You can limit your opportunities to meet new people, explore new places, and have new experiences. But by limiting yourself to the familiar, you also limit your happiness. An old adage tells us that variety is the spice of life. But there is little variety in the known. It's the same old drag day after day.

Fear of the unknown is groundless. The unknown is exactly that, unknown. You do not know what the future will bring, so why should you be afraid of it? Even if you did know that something bad was going to happen to you at a future time, would your fear prevent it from happening? No. All your fear will do is to prevent you from living a happy and healthy life now. It will immobilize you and prevent you from dealing with the challenges in your life. Remember, it is impossible for you to avoid the unknown. You are surrounded by it, and you yourself are part of it. Throw aside your groundless fear of the unknown, and begin to explore it. It is only in the unknown that you will find the answers to your needs.

Staying with the known is more harmful than journeying into the unknown, and more boring too. Explore the unknown with courage! You'll discover that there was really nothing to be afraid of, after all.

The greatest fear of the unknown is the fear of death. Surveys have indicated that the fear of death creates more stress and anxiety than any other fear. Like all other fears, it prevents a person from enjoying his present life. The fear of death will not prolong your life. If anything, it will only hasten your death by bringing you into a dangerous state of stress.

Why are people afraid of death? Because death is the symbol of the unknown, and because there is so much mystery about the process of dying. We human beings live on a little island which we call life. Life is the island of the known, and we are surrounded by an infinite ocean of the unknown, which we call death.

The primary cause of the fear of death is the belief that death is an unnatural process. In fact, death is as natural as life. All things that are born must die. So what is there to fear? *Never fear that which is inevitable.* It is a waste of your energy.

The first step in overcoming your fear of death is to accept death as both inevitable and natural. Death is part of the cycle of life. If we examine the world of nature, we see that all living creatures go through a seven-stage cycle consisting of conception, birth, growth, maturation, decay, and death. Death, in short, is part of life itself. It is not something that is abnormal or unusual. We have attached so many foolish fears to the idea of dying that it has become a potent producer of stress in our society. The truth is, we have absolutely no evidence to suggest that death is any worse than life is. The idea that death is unnatural has been given strength by the way our society treats persons who are terminally ill. From man's advent on earth, until about fifty years ago, most people died at home, surrounded by their families and friends. Dying at home in surroundings they knew, helped a dying person to relax and accept his oncoming death more easily. It also gave children and other adults the opportunity to see what dying was like.

But today we cart our loved ones off to the hospital and let them die with strange people in sterile and unfamiliar surroundings. These conditions are sufficient to induce a high state of stress even in a healthy person, let alone in someone who is ill, in pain, and who is trying to prepare himself for death. This process also creates a mystique about both death and doctors. We grow up thinking that death is unnatural because we don't see it taking place. We hand over all responsibility to the doctor, falsely believing he knows something about death that we don't. If we would allow people to die at home instead of in hospitals, then we would see that death *is* a natural part of existence. Consider for a moment. Would you rather die in a hospital room or at home? The choice is yours.

Religion and philosophy have enabled millions of persons to assuage their fears of death. Most religions affirm the idea that each person has a soul that will survive after clinical death has occurred. Some religions teach that the soul will go to an afterworld, while others affirm that the soul will return to this earth for another life. If you subscribe to any of these systems, then you should not fear death. If you believe in an afterlife, then think of death as the next step in your growth and development, a step which you are not taking alone. If you believe in God, then feel that God will be with you at the time of your death. God will protect you and guide you on your journey into the unknown. Your belief in God can easily nullify your fears of death. Don't think of death as the end, but as a new beginning.

If you do not believe in God or in an afterlife, then think of death as rest. A lifetime on earth is a lifetime of struggle. Death provides rest and a release from that struggle. Don't overestimate the importance of death. It is just another step in your journey. And don't force yourself to disbelieve in an afterlife. Leave yourself open to the possibility. Who knows? You may be pleasantly surprised.

Death can help you overcome your other fears and worries if you will allow it to. One reason people allow themselves to enter into negative psychological states is because they feel that they have all the time in the world at their disposal. By putting the thought of death out of their minds, they fool themselves into thinking that there is no need to hurry. If you think that you will be here forever, then why worry about being happy today; you still have tomorrow. But thinking about your death can help you overcome mental and physical lethargy. If you found out that you were going to die in six months, what effect would it have on you? After you had overcome your initial shock, you would probably decide to live your life to the fullest. You wouldn't allow yourself to indulge in useless fears and worries. They would all seem too trivial to bother with in the light of your oncoming death. In the same sense, your awareness of your own mortality can help you to eclipse your other fears. It is possible for you to die at any moment. Don't assume that death is going to occur at the time you think it will.

You can use this truth to live a better and fuller life. If you are aware that the possibility of death is always with you, then you can stop putting off life. You are probably like most people in that you always assume that tomorrow you will have time for the things you want, or that tomorrow you will finally become happy, relaxed, and enjoy life. But death may not give you a tomorrow. So, throw away your *mañana* philosophy and start living today. Use death as an advisor to help you. Each time you become worried, tense, or upset, ask yourself: "Is this really worth allowing myself to become upset over? My death may come at any time. I have to live and be happy now. Why should I allow this to upset me?" In the light of your death it is totally insignificant. Be happy here and now.

Fear of Change

Don worked for a large clothing retailer in Chicago. He was in charge of designing all of the displays for the store he worked in. He was happily married, had four children, and lived in the suburbs. Don was good at his job and enjoyed the people he worked with. His salary was not as large as he would have liked, but he and his wife always managed to make ends meet.

Don had never been in a rush to climb up his company's ladder. He liked to work, but he also enjoyed spending free hours at home with his family. As a result, he was passed over for several promotions. Then he was transferred to another of the company's stores in a different section of town. At the new store, his job was not as challenging. Also, Don and his co-workers disliked the manager of the store. Don thought about leaving his job, but couldn't because he was afraid to change his circumstances.

Don knew that he had to keep a steady supply of money coming in. While he didn't particularly like his new job, he felt that it was relatively safe. He had been with the company for a number of years and he believed that he would never be fired. He feared that if he got a job with a different chain of department stores, the job might not last, and then what would he do? He decided to accept his situation and avoid change.

But the combined stress from his dissatisfaction with his job and working with his new boss started to tell on Don. He became irritable, tense, and oversensitive. He argued with his wife and yelled at his children without meaning to. He was subject to fits of depression which he unsuccessfully tried to hide. He was almost on the verge of a nervous collapse when he attended a Total Relaxation Seminar. During the seminar, I spoke with Don about his fears, and tried to show him that his fear of change was gradually destroying him. Once he realized that fact, he quit his job, found another job he liked better, and the lines of worry and anxiety that had been creeping into his face began to disappear.

If you are perfectly happy with your job, then there is certainly no reason to change it. Making changes simply for the sake of changes is not a good idea. But when you feel that you are getting into a rut, or that you are no longer challenged by your job, it is time to move forward. Staying, when it is time to go, places you under unnecessary stress and tension.

The fear of change is similar in many ways to fear of the unknown, and you should apply the same rules for defeating it. Your enemy is not change. Change is good for you. When faced with changing circumstances in your life, you reach deeper within yourself and unleash more of your hidden talents and abilities. Don't sell yourself short. You are capable of much more than you imagine. But only change will cause you to bring out your full potential. It is not change that is bad for you, but the fear of change.

Fear of change prevents you from doing many of the things that you would enjoy doing. Fear of change can prevent you from changing your career, getting married, getting divorced, trying new types of food, getting a different type of car, and so on. Realize that change is good for you, and that it is only your immobilizing and pointless fear of change that is bad for you. With this attitude, and by using the Total Relaxation Problem-Solving Formula when necessary, you will easily be able to defeat your fear of change forever.

Divorce and Separation

There is an erroneous assumption built into our culture that marriage is good and divorce is bad. The effects of this assumption can be clearly seen if you observe someone getting married and another person who is in the process of getting a divorce. From a logical standpoint, a person getting a divorce should be under less stress than someone who is getting married. A person who is getting married is entering into a totally unfamiliar lifestyle, whereas a person getting a divorce is simply returning to a lifestyle similar to one he had before.

The reason that divorce creates so much stress is twofold. On the one hand, a person is going against the unwritten moral judgments of our twentieth-century tribal community. While divorces have become much more frequent in the last fifty years, our ingrained puritan heritage still tells us that divorce is not good. But the second and greater cause of strain in a divorce or separation is the fear of change. Because of the fear of change, many persons who *should* get divorced stay bound to someone they either no longer love, or simply can't get along with.

For many years a person lives happily by himself. Then he meets someone, falls in love, and gets married. After sharing many experiences together, one or both partners may find that they are no longer happy in their marriage. They may still love each other, but loving someone does not always mean that you will like him or be able to live comfortably with him. At this point, they should shake hands, wish each other luck, and part as friends. But, unfortunately, this is not usually the case.

You have chosen the person you are married to above all others. Just because you can no longer live together in harmony is no reason to dislike or hate the person you loved the best.

Staying in a stagnant marriage or relationship places a tremendous burden of stress upon yourself and your partner. You begin to become frustrated and angry with each other. All you succeed in doing by staying together, when the time has really come to go your own ways, is to destroy all of the beauty you shared together. The primary force responsible for people staying together when they should separate is the fear of change.

People mask their fear of change with a variety of excuses. One or both partners will wistfully look at each other and, after thinking about all of the "good" times they have shared together, they will decide not to part. Or they will tell themselves (or each other) that they simply can't live without each other. What nonsense! It sounds like a rejected script from a television soap opera. Now these two will proceed to make each other miserable for the rest of their lives, when they could have each gone their own way and had a happy and fulfilling existence.

Staying together with someone because of the "good times" you have experienced in the past is pointless and illogical. The past is dust. No matter how wonderful those good times were, they no longer exist. When you were having those "good times" together, were you having them because you were held together by the memory of past "good times"? No, of course not. You were living in that present moment and enjoying it together. This is a new moment. If you use it correctly, it will bring you even "better times" than you had before. But if you tie yourself to a relationship that you have outgrown, then you will prevent the better times of the present from occurring. Clinging to the past is only an excuse for avoiding your fear of change. Recognize your fears and conquer them. Then begin a new and happier life by yourself again.

Much of the stress that women and men experience when they contemplate separation or divorce is brought on by their fears of being alone. Again we must deal with one of our society's false equations:

$$\frac{\text{Being Alone}}{\text{Loneliness}} = \frac{\text{Unhappiness and Guilt}}{\text{Fear (what will happen to me?)}}$$

If you are like most people, you probably don't know too much about being alone. Our society teaches us that there is something inherently wrong with being alone. The unspoken premise is that people are alone because they are unwanted. This idea is reinforced by both the advertising and the entertainment fields. Rarely do you see people on television shows or in commercials who are having a wonderful time being by themselves. Unfortunately, our society equates togetherness with happiness.

From a verbal point of view, the words lonely and alone

are very similar. Yet being by yourself is an essential element in learning to relax and in getting more out of life. As
long as you are constantly surrounded by others, it is very
difficult to get in touch with yourself. Unless you can get in
touch with yourself, you will never have a true sense of what
it is you want from your life. Being by yourself for short
periods of time is essential to your growth and development.
But being by yourself does not mean taking along your radio,
television, or telephone. It means you, by yourself, with
yourself. Getting to know yourself. A very pleasant idea.

To overcome your fear of being alone, learn to enjoy being
alone. When you are by yourself, enjoy yourself. Read a book,
paint a picture, try being a creative cook, meditate, take a
walk, jog, or just sit quietly and enjoy the silence. Then, after
you have spent enough time being with yourself, visit a
friend.

Living by yourself enables you to have the space you want
when you need it. The fear of living alone stems from the
false idea that something awful will happen to you if there is
not someone around to take care of you. A common fear in
this genre is: "But suppose I get sick and no one is there to
take care of me?" This is a popular excuse for staying with
someone you are no longer happy with. But when was the
last time you needed to have someone watch over you when
you were sick? Probably not since you were a child. If you are
ill, call a friend. She'll be glad to drop by to make sure you're
all right.

If you still are not convinced that you would like living
alone, and you insist on creating stress and tension for you
and your partner by keeping a bad marriage together, then
consider moving in with a roommate. If you don't know
someone, then ask around. In most cities there are services
that screen and match roommates. Don't allow your fear of
the unknown to bind you to a bad marriage or other relationship. Act with courage. If you really love someone, you
will not place him under the constant stress which comes
from the bickering and hurt feelings of a marriage that is

past its prime. If your partner doesn't have the strength to take the first step, then you take it. For both of your sakes.

Did I hear someone ask: "But what about the children?" Well, what about them? Do you think that living in a home that is a hotbed of tension and unrest is going to make them happy and healthy? Children who grow up in a stressful environment often become emotionally handicapped. They learn to imitate Mom and Dad, which means they learn their responses to stress. Children are not naive. You can't fool them by not arguing in front of them. They *feel* everything that goes on. If you really love your children and are concerned for their happiness and well-being, then bring them up in a stress-free environment. If your marriage is creating constant stress, do your children a favor; don't use them as an excuse for failing to confront your own fear of change.

Try a trial separation and see how you feel. Expect to experience a temporary rise in stress at the start of this separation. But wait and see. You will discover that living alone is not lonely. Experiment with your life.

Don't put off being happy today for uncertain happiness tomorrow. If you expect that your marriage is going to suddenly get better and blossom, you are entering into the expectation trap. Some people spend their whole lives waiting for a change that never comes. Evaluate your situation. If you have no reason to suspect a dramatic and permanent change, then act with courage and change your situation.

Fear of Pain

Many persons experience a great deal of anxiety because they are afraid of pain. The fear of pain, like all other fears, is a useless emotion. When you are afraid of pain, you place yourself in an overwrought emotional state which will actually *intensify* your pain by making you more conscious of it. At the same time, you experience unnecessary stress, which can only result in further damage to your body.

The anticipation of pain can often be more painful than the physical pain that follows. A classic view of the fear of pain is provided in *Alice in Wonderland* when Alice is speaking with the Queen:

> Alice was just beginning to say, "There's a mistake somewhere—" when the Queen began screaming so loud that she had to leave the sentence unfinished. "Oh, oh, oh!" shouted the Queen, shaking her hand about as if she wanted to shake it off. "My finger's bleeding! Oh, oh, oh, oh, oh!"
>
> Her screams were so exactly like the whistle of a steam-engine that Alice had to hold both hands over her ears.
>
> "What *is* the matter?" she said, as soon as there was a chance of making herself heard. "Have you pricked your finger?"
>
> "I haven't pricked it *yet*," the Queen said, "but I soon shall—oh, oh, oh!"

Pain is, to some extent, unavoidable. But a knowledge of what pain is, and how to deal effectively with it, will enable you to eliminate your fear of pain and minimize any actual pain that you suffer. For purposes of a simple definition, let us say that pain is your body's warning signal that some type of damage is being done to you. As a rule, pain itself will not damage you in any way. But your fear of pain will. When you experience pain, try to lessen any pressure that may be increasing your pain. Then, if you are unsure of the cause of your pain, or if it requires treatment, contact a doctor or other qualified person. Remain calm. Getting upset will not help you overcome your pain. It will only cause you to lose your proper perspective and, in the resulting confusion, you may only injure yourself further.

Do not ignore your pain! Pain is your body's warning signal. If you heed your body's warnings, you can prevent further possible damage. If your pain was caused by a minor injury that does not require treatment, then simply try to ignore it. But if your pain is severe, have it treated. Thanks to modern medical techniques and new drugs, most types of pain can either be eliminated or greatly reduced. The idea that experiencing pain and suffering will make you a better person is absurd. Avoid pain when you can. When you can't, do not be afraid of it. Remember, your fear will only make matters worse, not better. If you must experience pain, then use one of the following two strategies to help lessen your pain.

● Going Above Pain. When you are faced with unavoidable pain, whether it is from a visit to the dentist's office, from arthritis, or from some other ailment, divert your attention from your pain. Thinking about your pain will only make it seem worse. Rise above your pain by using any of the Total Relaxation Core Techniques. Ignore your pain and focus all of your attention on the technique. You will find that you will be able to lessen your awareness of your pain in this way.

● Going Into Pain. Another method of dealing with pain is to focus your attention directly on it. This method is only for the brave, and should not be used as a substitute for effective medical treatment.

When you focus your attention on the pain, use all of your concentrative powers. Take your awareness and enter into your pain completely. Follow it to its source. If you can keep your attention focused completely upon the pain, you will discover that pain, in its essence, is only sensation.

Throughout your life, you have experienced a variety of sensations. Those sensations that you like, you refer to as pleasurable; those sensations that you dislike, you classify as pain. But ultimately pleasure and pain are raw physical sensations. If you focus all of your attention on either, then you will be able to see pleasure and pain in a new light. From this new vantage point you will see that pain is not pain, and pleasure is not pleasure. Both are sensations which you can choose to ignore.

Remember, if you have any doubt about the pain, consult a doctor. These two strategies are not going to help you overcome the cause of your pain. They will help you mentally remove yourself from your pain, but that is all. They are not to be considered as any form of medical treatment.

Fear of Yourself

Fear of yourself doesn't mean looking in the mirror and getting frightened. Fear of yourself is your inability to accept yourself as you are. It stems from a general lack of knowledge about who you are and what it is you want to become.

Many people feel that there is something wrong with them. They don't really want to know who or what they are because they are afraid that if they take a good look at themselves they will be disappointed. They fear that they will discover they are nothing but a mass of imperfections. This type of fear is totally unfounded and unnecessary. In order to overcome it, an individual must realize that imperfections are not important, perfection is important. Everyone has weaknesses. But a person who is afraid of himself is convinced that his weaknesses are more important than his strengths.

Forget your imperfections. Thinking about your weaknesses will not make them go away. Brooding about your weaknesses will only make them stronger. Instead, concern yourself with perfection. By thinking about the good qualities that you already possess, you will be inspired to improve yourself. If you have a low opinion of yourself, you are wrong. You are a wonderful, valuable, and sensitive human being. You have the ability to overcome your imperfections, to turn your weaknesses into strengths, and to make your current strengths stronger. Do not be afraid of yourself. There is no imperfection that cannot be overcome with some hard work, guidance, and patience.

The fear of failure is one imperfection which can be overcome. Fear of failure will prevent you from living a happy, stress-free life. Your constant anxiety over failure will only place you in a negative psychological state and pave the way for nervous tension. If you want to eliminate your fear of failure, then you have to gain a new understanding of what failure is. As long as you feel that failure is shameful, damaging, painful, or destructive, you will be afraid of it. Feel that failure is a natural part of the growth cycle. It is not a final end in itself. In the process of learning to walk, a child will often stumble and fall down. But once he learns to walk, he doesn't feel that stumbling was a failure. He understands that it was a natural part of the process of learning how to walk.

If you think of failure as something that is molding, shaping, and teaching you, then you will not be afraid of it. Your fear of failure only comes when you assume that you will never succeed. All great men and women have experienced failure. Their greatness does not stem from the fact that they never failed. Their greatness came about because they accepted failure as a necessary part of the learning process. They were not discouraged by it. They didn't keep doing the same wrong things over and over. They learned from their failures and continued to make progress. They realized that if they allowed their fear of failure to prevent them from trying, it would be impossible for them to succeed.

Eliminate the word failure from your vocabulary. If someone else tells you that you have failed, it is only his limited judgment and assessment of your abilities. There is only one type of failure, and that is when you give up. As long as you are trying to overcome your limitations, you can never be considered by yourself, or anyone else who truly understands the nature of success and failure, as a failure.

Always take failure as an experience. Do not take it as a finished product or as the culmination of an experience. If you think that failure is the end of your experience, then you are mistaken. Do not measure your success or failure in terms of the expectations of yourself or others. What is important is not your so-called failure, but what you learned from it. Remember, slow and steady wins the race. Accept failure not as defeat, but as a sign that you are trying and therefore making progress.

The fear of success is directly related to the fear of failure. If you fear success, it is because you feel that once you have succeeded, you will have to continue to succeed. You must learn not to make too much out of success. Success, like failure, is just another step in the learning process. Be encouraged by both your successes and failures, but don't be afraid of them.

Many people are afraid of success because they feel that once they have achieved success they will only go downhill. This is a fallacy. If, for example, you were an athlete and you achieved success while you were in your twenties, does that mean, if you can no longer perform as well in your thirties or forties, that you are a failure? No, of course not! In your life you will have many so-called victories and defeats. But the real victor is the person who is constantly able to overcome personal limitations and who can help others do the same. Don't measure your success or failure by what you do or achieve in life. Measure your success by what you become.

Some individuals fear success because they are afraid of the added demands and responsibilities it often brings. However, it is only through accepting responsibilities that we can grow. A weightlifter lifts heavy weights in order to develop his muscles. As he lifts progressively heavier weights, his muscles become larger. In the same sense, as you shoulder more responsibility, you will find that you will become stronger inwardly. Responsibility, when properly used, will make you stronger so that you can win the greatest victory of all, the victory over your own doubts, worries, tensions, fears, and insecurities. Don't be afraid of success. If you gain added responsibility from success, accept it as a tool with which you can further your own development. Remember that the only real success is your own constant development as a happy, healthy human being. Allow success and failure to work for you, not against you.

The Fear of Fear

Don't be afraid of dealing with your fears. If you are afraid of your fears, then you will never overcome them. The best medicine for overcoming your fears is courage. If you are timid about conquering your fears, they will defeat you.

What you need is a new approach to conquering your problems. Being afraid will never help you in this respect. If you want to conquer your fears, you have to confront them with courage, patience, and perseverance. This is the only way you will overcome them on any lasting basis.

If you know how to look at a problem, then half the strength of that particular problem will go away. But most people try to avoid a problem by running away from it. When something unfortunate happens to you in your life, you should not think that it has come about because you have done something wrong. By blaming yourself and trying to hide, you will not solve your problems. First you must face your problem and see if you are to blame. If somebody else is creating the problem, then you have to be very strong and prevent him from affecting you. If you yourself are the problem, then only by taking the time to learn more about yourself and by developing your inner strengths will you be able eventually to overcome your inadequacies.

When you apply the Problem-Solving Formula to the fear of fear, or any other life problem, you will be able to deal with it more effectively. Confront your fear, analyze it, and take the necessary action to overcome it. By applying this strategy, you will be able to overcome any fear, however strong it may be.

Strategies for Overcoming Fear

● Nothing beneficial ever comes from fear. Fear is the chief cause of psychological stress. It will cause you to enter into dangerous states of anxiety and tension.

● Realize that there is nothing wrong with you, and that you have the power within you to overcome your fears.

● Don't be concerned with your fears, but with your strengths.

● Untended fears only grow stronger. If you try to hide and run away from your fears, they will follow you.

● Confront your fears. Remember that the best medicine for overcoming your fears is courage. Within you is a limitless supply of courage. But you have to exercise your will power to draw upon it.

● Don't be afraid of the unknown. Accept the unknown as a friend and helper.

● Accept change as a natural part of life. Remember, no change = no growth. Ride the changes of your life like a surfer riding a wave. Allow the changes to move you forward in life.

● Never be afraid of your successes and failures. Success and failure are necessary parts of the learning process.

● There is only one real failure in life, and that is when you give up. Never give up! Regardless of how slow your progress may be, it is taking you towards your goal.

● Being afraid of pain intensifies your pain. Confront pain and see that it is nothing to fear. Your fear of pain will hurt you far more than pain itself.

The Destructive Aspects of Doubt

The third major cause of psychological stress is self-doubt. Self-doubt is the cause of insecurity and many other stress-related ailments. Self-doubt causes you to lose control of your emotions and inner peace faster than any other factor. Take the following case of self-doubt.

Bob was the manager of a large New York City advertising firm. Most people assumed from his appearance that he was happy, self-confident, and fulfilled. He was a success in business, had an active social life, and on the surface had what appeared to be a good relationship with his wife and three children.

But, unknown to anyone but Bob and his wife, he had constant self-doubts. They caused him to experience tremendous tension and anxiety. As a result, it was very difficult for him to sleep at night, and to enjoy almost any of the activities he participated in.

Bob's self-doubt expressed itself in many ways. He always felt at work that he was just getting by. He doubted he was really capable of doing as good a job as other men in his field. He believed that he had got the job by luck, and he doubted whether he could get another good job if he lost his present one.

Bob also doubted his intelligence. This was difficult for his friends and business acquaintances to understand, because on the surface he was smooth and well informed. Bob had as much formal education as his friends, but he constantly compared himself to them and, in his own mind, he felt they were superior to him.

The only person who was aware of Bob's battle with his self-doubts was his wife. She saw the other side of his character, which was revealed each night when he came home. After work, Bob would withdraw into himself. He constantly found fault and criticized his wife, children, and his friends. But Bob's criticisms were not justified. They were merely a psychological ploy which he used to project what he suspected were his own limitations, onto others. By criticizing and finding fault with others, he was attempting to take the blame off himself. His unconscious logic was simple: "If I see that everyone else is imperfect, then my imperfections will not annoy me as much."

The tragedy of Bob's life was that he was capable, intelligent, and even gifted. But his self-doubts, although completely unfounded, were so strong that they prevented him from being happy. They caused him to become so tense that he eventually had a massive heart attack and lost his job.

If Bob had been able to realize the futility of his self-doubts, then his life, and the lives of his wife and children, would have been happier. In Bob's case, and to an extent in the lives of most people, self-doubt plays a strong role in creating unnecessary stress, tension, and unhappiness.

Overcoming Self-Doubt

The first step in overcoming self-doubt is to realize how useless it is. Nothing, *nothing* productive ever comes from self-doubt. Self-doubt immobilizes you and prevents you from acting and achieving on the levels you are capable of. Self-doubt gives birth to an overall defeatist, "sour grapes" attitude.

When you doubt yourself, who is the loser? No one else but you. Self-doubt only prevents you from seeing what you have and what you are. When you doubt yourself, you immediately stop yourself before you start. If, for example, you doubt you could be a good tennis player, why should you even try? It's much easier to sit at home feeling sorry for yourself than to get out on the court and see how well you can do. If you doubt that you can succeed in any field, whether it is in business, athletics, the arts, or self-development, you will automatically defeat yourself.

You have no idea what you can become or do. You only know what you have been able to do and become in the past. But that was yesterday; who knows what you are capable of today? Just because you did not succeed at something in the past does not mean that you will not in the future. Remember, nothing productive or positive will ever come out of self-doubt. Self-doubt will only create dangerous states of tension, anxiety, and worry within you. Throw your doubt away. It's too heavy a burden for you to carry!

It doesn't cost anything to believe in yourself. And even if it did, do you know of a better investment than you? By learning to believe in yourself, you will be able to do and achieve more of the things you want, and you will put a permanent end to the stresses and tensions caused by your self-doubt.

In order to believe in yourself, it is first necessary to like yourself. Go take a look in the mirror. That person staring back at you is your best friend. You might as well learn to like him now, because you are going to be with him for the rest of your life.

You will like yourself better when you become what you

know you are capable of. As long as you allow your problems to overwhelm you and you don't do the things you know you should, you will find it difficult to respect yourself. You must be true to yourself under all circumstances and conditions. When you are true to yourself, then and only then will you be happy.

Being true to yourself doesn't mean living up to the expectations of your family, friends, and society. In order to be true to yourself, you will have to turn aside from conventionality and blaze new paths into the unknown. Don't worry about fulfilling the expectations of others. Simply actualize all of your abilities. The sign of how true you are to yourself is the amount of personal growth you achieve every day. Each day when you learn something new, overcome a limitation, and grow, you are being true to yourself. Happiness is a prerequisite for relaxation. Unhappy people are tense, nervous, and afraid. Take the short cut to happiness and be true to yourself. Form a fan club of one. Learn to like you.

If you find it hard to believe in yourself, then try imagining that you believe in yourself. Imagination is a powerful tool that you can use to overcome any problem. In our society, we often think of imagination as something illusory or unreal. But we should not confuse imagination with daydreaming or fantasizing.

Without imagination, it is virtually impossible to do or become anything. If you could not imagine yourself getting out of bed in the morning, then you would probably stay there forever. If you want to invent a new recipe, start a business or corporation, buy a house, get married, close an important business deal, or do almost anything, it is necessary to imagine it happening before you do it. No imagination, no creation—that's the rule.

Use your imagination to help you defeat self-doubt or any other limitation. Spend a few minutes each day imagining yourself as you would like to be. If you lack self-confidence and are overwhelmed by doubt and insecurity, then picture yourself without these negative qualities. Mentally create a visual image of yourself as a confident, happy, doubt-free person. Then use your insights and energy to throw your doubts away and become what you have imagined. Let imagination be the first step in creating the new you. The other steps will follow in rapid succession.

If you are afraid of change or the unknown, then imagine yourself as a courageous person who welcomes the opportunities for growth that change and the unknown bring. If you are constantly plagued by worries, then imagine yourself as a person who is worry-free. For a few minutes each day, think of yourself as you would like to be. Through the creative use of your imagination you will begin rapidly advancing in the direction of your choice.

TOTAL RELAXATION TECHNIQUE #3
THE OCEAN

Imagine a vast ocean. The ocean is filled with hundreds and thousands of waves. Feel that you are part of that ocean. Imagine that each wave in the ocean is slowly moving through you. Feel that each wave is a wave of joy. Imagine wave after wave of joy passing through your whole body. As each wave passes through your body, feel that all worries, tensions, anxieties, and problems are being washed away in the successive waves of joy. For several minutes, imagine wave after wave of joy passing through you. Feel that each wave of joy that passes through you increases the amount of joy that you now have, until you feel that you have become all joy. Nothing exists for you except limitless, boundless joy.

Now imagine that you are going beneath the surface of the ocean. The surface of the ocean is filled with many waves, but below the surface, in the depths, all is calm, silent, and serene. Imagine yourself sinking slowly into the depths of the ocean. Here there is only calmness, quiet, and tranquility. As you imagine yourself going deeper and deeper into the depths of the ocean, feel that peace is entering into you. Feel that the deeper you go into the inner ocean, the more peaceful and calm you become. Feel that there is no end to the depths of this ocean. It goes on endlessly. Imagine yourself sinking deeper and deeper into the endless ocean, feeling more peace and more tranquility filling your entire being until you have become all peace, and all tranquility.

Four

Overcoming
Environmental Stress

When any real progress is made, we unlearn and
learn anew what we thought we knew before.
— HENRY DAVID THOREAU: *Journals*

You are a victim of environmental stress. Every day you
are adversely affected by a variety of environmental stresses
that are steadily draining away your health and happiness
when you are in your home, going to and from work, while
you are at work, and during your leisure time and holidays.
Through the application of the strategies and Total Relaxation techniques in this chapter, you will be able to overcome
environmental stress in these specific areas and restore the
natural relaxation balance which is necessary for your continued health and happiness.

Environmental stress is a by-product of our modern way of
life—the price we are paying for poor planning and resources
management, radical shifts in technology, and a general lack
of awareness of the needs of individual members of society.
One of the most pressing concerns affecting you is the energy
crisis, which has placed you under a plethora of stresses
ranging from waiting in gas lines to paying higher prices for
everything you purchase. Let us hope that a day will dawn
when the human race learns to minimize the unnecessary
stress it creates for itself. But for those of us who are here
now, and for our children and our children's children, environmental stress is a real and deadly threat.

The answer to overcoming environmental stress is

twofold. We must begin to think of the future. Unless we begin to rethink and change our value systems and lifestyles, we are headed for a world crisis the likes of which humanity has never known before. If we can learn from our past mistakes and explore new pathways, it will be possible for us to thwart the constant encroachment of environmental stress, and once again make our world a pleasant and fruitful place to live. In the meantime, there are steps you can take to minimize the environmental stresses that attack you each day. The best place to begin the battle is within your own territory.

Environmental Stress and Your Territory

A number of anthropological studies have shown that the primary drive within man and many animals is the drive to secure a territory. This territorial imperative causes each human being instinctively to lay claim to a specific area of his own. When an individual's territory is invaded, or any attempt is made to dislodge him from his territory, he immediately enters into a severe state of stress.

In several experiments, laboratory animals were provided with ideal breeding conditions in controlled spaces. As the animal population increased, each respective member of the animal community had less and less territory. When overcrowding occurred, all the animals within the community showed signs of severe stress. Even though there were adequate food supplies, many of the animals stopped eating and eventually died. Animals who had not displayed aggressive tendencies prior to a reduction of their territory began to attack other members of their community without provocation. Many of the animals lost their sex drives, or began to demonstrate homosexual tendencies. All of the animals were more prone to disease and had a reduced life span.

Your primary territory is your home. If you live alone, your entire house or apartment can be considered as your territory. If you share your home with others, you live in a group territory.

If you live with others, then each member of your household claims a portion of your domicile as his or her own territory. As long as the members of your household respect each other's territorial boundaries, they do not place each other under territorial stress. However, when they violate each other's space, they upset the balance of your household and place *all* of the members of your living unit under stress.

Throughout the history of the human race the family unit ensured the territorial rights of the individual members of the family. Each member of the family knew what his or her place was and respected the territorial rights of the other members. But owing to the restructuring of the family unit that has occurred within the last fifty years, individual family members are no longer sure what their territory is. The changing roles of men and women have created a kind of territorial overlap. Since more women are now working, and more men are sharing in the household duties, the kitchen, which was once considered the inviolable domain of the woman of the house, is now also the territory of the man. The den or study, which was considered the territory of the man, is now also the territory of the woman. There is no question that these are good and necessary changes. But since each individual feels a powerful instinctual need for a territory of his or her own, and no substitute territories have yet been worked out, members of the typical modern household are constantly violating each other's traditional territories and placing each other under stress and tension.

Since the modern living unit is so conducive to stress, you must consciously deal with the question of territory in your own home. Whether you live in a house, apartment, condominium, mobile home, houseboat, or tent, everyone in your household should have a room, or part of a room that is his. Even if it is only an area around a person's bed, it should be recognized as his or her private area and should only be entered with their permission. Each member of your household should be responsible for the maintenance and decoration of that space. The privacy of each household member's territory should be respected, especially during hours when members of your household request that no one enter their space.

Strategies for Stress-Free Living Space

The following guidelines will help to ensure that you and the other members of your living unit do not subject each other to territorial stress.

● Have a family or living unit meeting and discuss the common and individual need for privacy for all of the members of your home. Find out if there are particular times when specific members of your household need their own space to relax in. For example, when you return from work, you may wish to be left alone until you have rested. By informing the others of your need, you will prevent them from unknowingly disturbing you.

● Assign each member of your household a room or space of his or her own. This is easiest when all household members have their own bedroom. But whether it's an entire room, or simply the area around their bed, it should be recognized as their own space which can only be entered with their permission.

● Avoid crowding together in one or two rooms when more rooms are available. If you know that there are times when members of your household need to use a specific room, as in the case of a bathroom or kitchen, try to allot specific times or time limits for its use. Few things can be more tension-provoking than being unable to get into the bathroom when you're late for work because someone is spending too much time in the shower. Discuss your common needs for shared space and make allowances for each other's needs.

● Beware of "media pollution" in your own space, and try not to allow your entertainment to violate the space of others. Not everyone has the same tolerance for noise, music, television, or the conversations of others. It is essential to recognize the different needs and sensitivities of one another if you are going to coexist peacefully. If the music from the next room is bothering you, don't wait until you boil over and start shouting. Inform the other person of the problem in a relaxed manner, and request that he or she turn the sound down.

● If someone has personal habits that you find annoying, speak to him. Internalizing your tension and frustration will only make you increasingly sensitive to those habits. Most people are flexible and will be glad to make allowances for your personal sensitivities. Don't assume that they can "read your mind" or know when they are annoying you. Speak up now so that you won't have to shout later.

● Don't infringe upon the space of your children and don't allow them to infringe upon your space. Reserve specific times for yourself and your spouse when your children *must* occupy themselves with their own interests. It will be impossible for you to appreciate your children if you are always with them.

● Don't feel that because someone doesn't want to be with you he or she is rejecting you. Realize that loving someone means leaving her alone when she wants to be alone. Be enough of a person to respect the rights of others' privacy without indulging in egotistical emotions. Spending time alone is important in maintaining good relationships. Respect the rights of others and they will freely offer their love and gratitude to you in return.

Commuting and Travel

According to a recent government survey, the average American worker spends sixty minutes traveling to and from work every day. The majority of Americans travel to work by car, bus, or train. A small percentage of the population travels to and fro on bicycles or on foot.

Early in the morning you leave your home and get into

your car. You then drive away from home and join the rapidly building stream of traffic commonly known as the morning "rush." During your morning and evening trip to and from work, you will make more decisions, and encounter more potential stress-causing situations, than you will during any equal time period of the day.

Occasionally, the traffic flows smoothly and you arrive at work without any difficulties. But most days, particularly if you live in one of the larger urban-metro areas of North America, the traffic jams and jams and jams.

Someone cuts you off, another driver is tailgating your car, horns blow all around you, you have a blowout on a busy highway, and then you end up sitting in a hopelessly snarled traffic jam wondering if you'll ever get out of it. Don't feel too bad. It's part of the madness of our modern world. Eventually the traffic will move, and if you allowed enough extra time when you left home, you might make it to work on time.

Unfortunately, it doesn't end on the highway. Once you have arrived at work that traffic jam is still going on inside your nervous system. The tension and frustration that you have internalized from your morning commute can put you on edge for the rest of the day. Despite your best intentions, you have become tense and overwrought. No wonder your day at work is less than satisfactory. And try as you might to forget, you know that the same traffic situations will be waiting for you after you finish work. The only difference will be that half the motorists on the road will be out there venting the tensions and frustrations they have built up during the day.

Some Strategies for Drivers

Getting mad and driving hard only increases your tension and sense of overall frustration. When you are tense and upset you are also more apt to make an error in judgment while driving. At fifty-five miles an hour you may not always survive such an error. In order to overcome stress when you commute and travel, utilize the following strategies:

• Don't drive too fast. Nothing makes the driver or passengers more tense than trying to make time. By driving a bit slower, you may lose ten minutes on an hour, but it won't take you an hour to unwind.

• Remain calm under all circumstances. If you find yourself starting to become tense and nervous when you are in a car, practice your affirmation (see Chapter three).

• Observe your body when you drive. Mentally check over your arms, legs, back, neck, and stomach to see if any of your muscles are tight or tense. If they are tense, then consciously relax them. The best drivers are always calm and relaxed. When something happens on the road that requires their immediate attention, their bodies respond automatically. But drivers who are keyed up and tense don't respond well to potential accident situations. They have exhausted their energy through their tension, and when the moment comes when they really need that energy, it has already been spent.

• If you are in a traffic jam, don't panic. If you are going to be late for work, for an appointment, or to catch a plane, you might as well relax and enjoy yourself. Worrying about whether or not you are going to be on time is not going to make the traffic in front of you go any faster. All it's going to do is ruin your day by making you tense and upset. Relax. Use your affirmation. Listen to some music you like. Think about your next vacation. Get your mind off the traffic jam. Thinking about it is not going to help.

• If you get caught in a traffic jam, accept it. Enter the lane that seems to be moving fastest and stay there. Don't lane hop. Studies of the California freeways have indicated that people who constantly hop lanes don't get there any faster. By lane hopping, you will only make yourself and other drivers more tense.

• Stay in full control of your vehicle. If talking to your passengers distracts you, then minimize your conversation. *Never* get in an argument with one of your passengers. You will become tense, angry, and more prone to losing control of your vehicle. If your passengers are doing something that annoys you, then politely ask them to stop. Don't feel that you shouldn't assert yourself because you may be hurting their feelings.

● On a three-lane highway or freeway, try to avoid driving in the far right lane. The entering and exiting traffic in this lane will cause you to speed up and slow down frequently, interrupting the flow of your driving.

● Avoid listening to loud music while driving. Try to listen to a station or a tape recording that has peaceful and relaxing music.

● When someone cuts you off or does something else equally thoughtless, resist the impulse to run them off the road. Simply ignore them. Getting mad at them won't help the level of your blood pressure, and it certainly won't change the way they drive. Without speeding, put as much distance between your car and their car as possible. That way you will avoid being bothered by their dangerous driving habits again.

● If your car won't start on your way to work or an appointment, don't waste your energy "freaking out." If you need to get to work quickly and your car shows no signs of starting, then leave it and find an alternate means of transportation. Don't worry about your car; you can make arrangements for its repair by phone later.

● If you do a lot of driving, it's a good idea to join the AAA or some other auto club that provides good road service. Then, if you have a breakdown at home or on the road, instead of dealing with an unknown service station which may overcharge you, you can call your auto club for assistance.

● If you have a breakdown on the road, stay calm. If you are on a local road, pull to the side and, provided it is safe to do so, leave your car and go seek assistance. If you are driving on a highway or other major road, it might be advisable for you to stay with your car. Pull off the highway if you can. If you are forced to leave your car on the highway, then, after turning on your car's emergency flashers or tying a white scarf to your antenna, get out and walk off the road to a safe location. Wait until help arrives.

● If you are involved in a traffic accident, don't panic. If you are in an accident, first check and see if you have been hurt. Then check to see if your passengers or the occupants of the other car have been injured. Most people panic in accident situations. But if you panic, a life may be lost. It is up to you to be the calm and relaxed person who will stabilize the situation. Your calmness will minimize the danger inherent in any accident.

● If you are a passenger in a car and the driver is making you tense because he is driving dangerously, speak to him and ask him to drive more carefully. If this doesn't work, find an alternate means of transportation.

● When children ride in your car, don't let them upset you. Explain to them that travel in an automobile is enjoyable, but serious too. If they persist in misbehaving, don't yell at them. Pull over to the side of the road until they are quiet. Then, when they are behaving properly, resume your journey.

Some Strategies for Passengers

● When you are on a crowded train or bus, use your affirmation (page 39).

● Occasionally check over your body for signs of tension. When you encounter tense muscles, consciously relax them. If you are very distressed, practice Total Relaxation Core Technique #4, "The Sphere of Power," which is given at the end of this chapter.

● If you want to avoid crowds, try going to work a little bit earlier. Often the train or bus that leaves just a few minutes before or after the one you usually take will have fewer people on it. Don't be a slave to habit. If you get to work a few minutes earlier, you may be able to get more done, or you will have an opportunity to relax for a few minutes before you start working.

● Make it a habit to bring something to read when you travel. Very often the environmental conditions of the buses and trains are unpleasant. The noises they make are disturbing, and the quality of the air is not the best. Reading or practicing any of the Total Relaxation Core Techniques can take your mind away from these inescapable environmental stresses. Being aware of them will only intensify their negative effect on you.

● If you have a very long or unpleasant commute, consider moving or changing jobs. You are not being paid for those extra hours during which you are subjecting yourself to additional environmental stress. Consider your options and don't stay with your job or continue living in the same old neighborhood because you are afraid of change or the unknown.

● Try commuting with a friend, or strike up a friendship with one of the regular commuters on your bus or train. It's much easier to while away your commuting time in pleasant conversation.

● If people are making you nervous because they are deliberately staring at you, simply ignore them. If they see that they are succeeding in upsetting you, they will continue. If you ignore them, they will eventually stop.

Environmental Stress at Work

Whether you work in an office, factory, store, at home, or in another setting, each day you are subjected to a variety of environmental stresses which can make you tense, worried, nervous, and fatigued. The causes of environmental stress will vary according to the type of employment you have. Some of the more common forms of environmental stress at work are: an unpleasant or noisy working atmosphere, an unfriendly boss or co-workers, pressure to produce faster, a change in your job responsibilities, competition from other employees or other businesses, inadequate salary, lack of concern on the part of your employer for your special problems, boredom, too much or not enough physical exercise on the job, constant traveling, and continual socialization with other employees or with clients.

In most cases it is impossible to eliminate stress while you are on the job. Since some environmental stress is present in all forms of employment, if you trade one job for another you will probably only be exchanging types of environmental stress. But if you can learn not to allow these stresses to get to you, you will effectively stop tension before it starts. You can easily do this by using the following 'Ideal' whenever you encounter environmental stress.

The Ideal

Form your Ideal by following the instructions in the next paragraph. Practice your Ideal several times before using it. Then, when tension, environmental stress, panic, fear, or worry strikes, ward it off by using your Ideal.

The Ideal is composed of two personal images which you can use to bring yourself into a calm and relaxed state of mind. To form the first image, search your memory for the time in your life when you feel that you were the happiest. Reflect for a minute or two upon the circumstances that surrounded or caused that happiness and jot down a brief description of them on a piece of paper.

To form the second image, call to mind a physical location where you have experienced great happiness and peace. (This should not be the location of the first image of your Ideal.) Write a brief description of that location down on the same piece of paper. Your two images will appear something like this:

My Ideal—Example #1

1. I was happiest the day I was married. All of my closest friends and relatives were there. It was a warm, beautiful day in May. The sun was shining and the birds were singing.

2. The place I have been happiest was my room as a child. I spent many wonderful hours playing there. I remember that the walls were blue, and that there were white curtains over the windows.

My Ideal—Example #2

1. I was happiest the first time I went skiing. It was cold and clear. I loved skiing down the slope, feeling the wind against my face. It was a special day and I will never forget it.

2. My favorite place is a beach in California near Big Sur. In the late afternoon the sun glistens on the columns of waves that crash against the black rocks. I always have feelings of freedom and exhilaration as I watch the white foam of the waves and smell the clean salt air.

After you have written down the two component parts of your Ideal, meditate upon them. First think for a moment about the time you were the happiest and try to reexperience part of that happiness. Then call to mind the second part of your Ideal, your favorite place. Visualize it. Although you may not have visited that location for some time, feel as though you are there now, happily enjoying yourself.

Allow your mind to alternate between these two images. You will find that with a little practice you can quickly and easily call the two images to mind. You will also discover that the more frequently you use your Ideal, the better it will work.

Working at Home

One of the most stressful occupations is the management of a household. If it is your job to manage a household, then you are responsible for shopping, cooking, cleaning, child care, and a variety of other tasks. In addition, many individuals also have outside jobs and careers. The combined effort of running a household and pursuing an outside career can be overwhelming.

One of the major forms of environmental stress that attacks people who manage households is boredom. The following list of strategies will help you overcome the stresses connected with working at home.

● Make it a point at least once a day to get out of the house. Go and visit a friend, go shopping, take time out for a walk or some other form of exercise, but above all, don't sit at home and brood.

● Try cleaning the house in a different way. If you always clean on a specific day, vary your schedule. If you normally clean the rooms of your home in a particular order, intentionally switch the order.

● If you can afford it, have someone come in to assist you with your housework once a week. Once he or she knows your cleaning routine, leave him alone and go enjoy yourself. But remember, if you spend all your time worrying about whether he is doing a good job or wondering if you are getting your money's worth, you are defeating the purpose of having someone help you.

● Let your husband or wife help you with cleaning or meal preparation. If you have children, assign them specific tasks like doing the laundry, carrying out the garbage, and so on. Give them enough responsibility to help them grow and to relieve you, without overburdening them.

● If you have small children and you have to spend most of your time with them, take them out occasionally. Children love adventure and are more rugged than you might suppose. Take them to museums, stores, parks, and other places of interest. If you are bored with your role as a parent, you will only become tense and irritable and affect your children in a negative way. Be a creative parent! Enjoy your children. Don't let them limit you; let them open new horizons for you. Learn to let your children's sense of wonder seep into your consciousness. As a rule, children aren't tense. Observe them and find out why.

● When the weather is bad, or if for some other reason you must be confined to your home for a long period of time, then start a new project. Learning is one of the best ways to end the tension produced by boredom. Try your local library. There are hundreds of books on fascinating subjects that you can learn from.

● If you watch television, instead of watching the same old shows or soap operas, try watching your local educational station. Remember, the important thing is stimulation. Too much time on your hands can cause tension and fatigue. Keep yourself active and busy doing beneficial things. Join a health spa, take some educational courses, do volunteer work for a charitable organization, or get a part-time job. Spend time with your friends and inspire each other to find constructive ways to broaden each other's horizons.

Job Hunting

If you are looking for a new job, have recently been fired or laid off, are looking for your first job, or are returning to the work force after an extended absence, you must prepare yourself to cope with a variety of environmental stresses that are indigenous to job hunting. The primary stresses that most persons encounter in their job search are: (1) the pressure to get a job within a limited amount of time; (2) the extraordinary fatigue that comes from the searching for employment; (3) filling out forms and questionnaires; and (4) personal interviews.

The following strategies will help you minimize environmental stress during your job hunt.

● Effectively organize your job campaign. Realistically

evaluate the type of job you are seeking and your own personal qualifications for that job. If you expect to get a job that you are not qualified for, or you expect to receive a larger salary than your qualifications merit, you are paving the way for stress with your unrealistic expectations.

● If you are unsure of your qualifications for a particular job, speak to an employment counsellor or someone who is already established in the field that you would like to enter. They will be able to give you constructive advice that will make your job search much easier and less stressful.

● Prepare yourself for exhaustion. Searching for a job may not require more hours than your normal workday does, but the hours you spend job hunting will require more energy and place you under environmental stresses that you are not accustomed to dealing with. You can reduce your fatigue by conserving energy during your job hunt. Allow yourself enough time between interviews or employment agencies to relax and take a break. If you have to wear special shoes for your interview which would be uncomfortable for a great deal of walking, bring a second pair of more comfortable shoes with you to wear in between interviews.

● Don't rush into a job simply because it's offered to you. Take your time and find a job that suits you. If you rush, you may find yourself unsuited to the job, and you may miss a much better opportunity that was waiting just around the corner.

● Before accepting a job, evaluate the apparent stress-causing factors that come with your new job and match them against your own tolerance for stress. If, for example, you don't smoke and you observe that most of the people in the office do, it might be wiser to find another place with more nonsmokers.

● Balance your potential pay scale against the amount of stress you will be subjected to on your new job. Remember that your paycheck will never compensate for any damage you suffer because of stress at work. Often the highest paying jobs will place you under the most stress. If your goals are not completely economic, consider taking another job that might pay slightly less but will not subject you to as much stress.

● Size up the people who will work above you, with you, and for you. Few things can induce more stress than a bad relationship with your boss, co-workers, or employees. If you feel that the "vibrations" of the people you will be working with are not good, look elsewhere.

● Budget your time efficiently, but give yourself extra time for unexpected changes in plans. If your time schedule is too tight, you will have problems if a potential employer keeps you waiting for an interview. Make it a point to leave early for an interview, allowing yourself extra time for dressing, make-up application, and travel. If you give yourself extra time, then, when your hair takes longer than you anticipated, you get stuck in a traffic jam, or your bus or train is late, it won't matter. But if you are tense and nervous because you are late, you will not be at your best during the interview.

● Practice one of the Total Relaxation Core Techniques before leaving for an interview or in a waiting room if you have extra time before your interview starts.

● Don't become frustrated when you fail to get a job in the amount of time that you think you should. Continue to persevere in a relaxed fashion. If you are not meeting with any success, talk to a professional job counsellor and follow his or her advice. They know the job market better than you do.

● Don't allow yourself to be frustrated by long or difficult questionnaires. Just deal with one question at a time. If you are unsure about what any of the questions mean or about the type of information you are supposed to supply, then ask the person who gave you the questionnaire. Don't become tense and overwrought because you are embarrassed to ask for help.

● Ask about salary, working conditions, and advancement possibilities during your interview. Don't wait until you get the job. An employer will be happy to answer your questions. He realizes what it is like to look for a job. Asking questions about your potential position and its range of responsibilities shows that you are interested in your work. By asking before you get the job, you can avoid tension and frustration later.

Retirement and Stress

After many years of leading an active and busy life, people leave their jobs and try to enjoy their remaining years pursuing their favorite activities. But unfortunately, most persons do not take into account the environmental stresses that are connected with retirement. As a result, these years are often marred by unnecessary worry, stress, tension, and boredom. The case of a New Jersey doctor illustrates this point.

Ira was a general practitioner who lived in Jersey City. During the course of their marriage, Ira and his wife never gave too much thought to their retirement years. The activities of their own and the childrens' lives consumed all their time. But when Ira reached sixty-two, he and his wife decided that it was time for him to give up his medical practice and move to Florida.

Ira had several friends who had retired to Florida and were very satisfied. Following their suggestions, he purchased a condominium in Boca Raton. After selling their New Jersey home, Ira and his wife moved to Boca and tried to acclimate themselves. But try as they might, they had little success.

After several days of fishing, Ira lost interest. He had never been an avid golfer so he and his wife tried sightseeing. But after visiting Disney World, the Miami Seaquarium, and the other tourist sights, they found that they were still unfulfilled. They surrendered themselves to a life centered around television, talking about their old life in New Jersey, and occasionally visiting their few friends in the area.

As the days turned into months, Ira became more tense and irritable. He discovered that Florida summers are unbearably hot, and he missed the change of seasons he was accustomed to in the North.

Finally, Ira admitted to his wife that they had made a mistake. Florida, he decided, was a nice place to visit but not retire to. They sold their condominium and moved back to New Jersey. Ira returned to a part-time practice and his wife started to take evening courses in Manhattan. Both of them found that they were much happier in the New York area.

Retirement Strategies

If you wish to minimize the stress of retirement, then utilize the following strategies:

● Do not go from a life of activity to a life of inactivity. Try to plan a variety of activities that are somewhat similar to those you now enjoy.

● If you find that you have too much time on your hands after retirement, consider part-time employment or volunteer work. Make new friends by joining clubs or by taking some educational courses.

● Don't let your children or friends push you into moving into a situation which you might find uncomfortable. Before moving to a new place, research it thoroughly. Stay in the area for a while and talk to local residents. The real estate or rental agent is not going to uncover the deficiencies of a community for you. Talk to people your own age whom you meet in the shops, and so on. Ask their opinions of the area and match their answers against your own particular needs.

● Don't think "old" before your time. You will only create unnecessary stress through boredom. A happy and relaxed life is a balance between stimulating activity and rest. Become as active as you can. This is your chance to explore life anew. But limit yourself to those activities you enjoy.

● Don't live your life backwards. Remember, the past is dust. Live in the present moment and look forward to the possibilities and adventures that each day brings.

● Don't spend too much time at home. This is one of the fastest ways to build up stress. Use the discounts that are given to senior residents of your community for the movies and other events in your area. Try exploring new hobbies. Take up painting, write a book, keep in touch with your friends. Keep active and busy. You'll be happier and more relaxed if you do.

● Avoid moving to a rest home or retirement village unless you are in need of the specialized services that they offer. These institutions are usually expensive and sterile. Often they create more stress than they alleviate.

One of the best ways to avoid boredom and to stay young is to associate with people younger than yourself. But in most retirement communities, you will only be surrounded by people your own age and older. Do not allow your relatives to push you into living in a retirement community. They are not the ones who will be living there, you are. If you are capable of living independently, then by all means do so. You will incur much less stress on your own than in a retirement community.

Leisure-Time Stress

Out of the one hundred and sixty-eight hours in a week, the average American devotes seventy-four hours to leisure-time pursuits. Theoretically, leisure time is spent relaxing and enjoying oneself. Unfortunately, many of the so-called leisure-time activities we participate in, such as sports, watching television, eating out, weekend activities, and parties, often create more stress and tension than they eliminate.

After Work Each Day

You are more susceptible to environmental stress after work each day than at any other time. At the end of your workday you are tired. You have been subjected to stress all day long and naturally your resistance to it is lower than it was earlier in the day. When you arrive home, you let your guard down, assuming that you will be able to throw away your tensions and relax. It is precisely at this time that you become the victim of the after-work tension formula.

Most people have unconsciously devised an after-work tension formula. When they return home they have a drink, eat a big meal, and spend a large part of their night watching television. Then they go to bed, have a poor night's sleep, and wake up groggy and tired the next morning. Each day that they repeat this formula, they lower their resistance to stress. It is no wonder that by the end of the work week most people are too tired and exhausted to really enjoy their weekends.

Understanding Media—Mainly Television.

The single greatest cause of tension and fatigue in the modern home is television. Your "boob tube" has earned its name well. As you while away your hours in front of it, you are subjecting your consciousness to a continual bombardment of useless stimuli that leave you feeling tired and unfulfilled at the end of the evening. You must come to terms with both the quantity and the quality of the programming you watch. If you don't, you are placing a negative energy drain upon yourself which will be hard for you to overcome.

I am not suggesting that you place an ad in the classified section of your local paper and sell your T.V. Far from it. But if you can understand what the effects of the "cool fire" really are, you may spend less time in front of it.

One of the primary reasons people in our culture experience so much stress and tension is that they do not know what real relaxation is. Most people make an unconscious equation between relaxation and sleep. They feel that the closer they can get to a sleeplike or drowsy state, the more relaxed they will be. But nothing could be farther from the truth. Relaxation is a state of balanced awareness in which you have overcome your worries, fears, and anxieties. Sleep relaxes and refreshes the body and mind—true. But if sleep were the cure for stress, all you would have to do would be to sleep more and you would be stress-free.

A certain amount of mental stimulation is necessary for the mind. Think of your mind as a muscle. A muscle that is underused becomes flabby and weak. A muscle that is constantly strained becomes taut and painful. But a muscle that receives both exercise and relaxation is in proper tone and balance. If you are a tense and nervous person, most of the day you are straining your mind with worries, negative thoughts, and false expectations. What your mind needs is to relax, refresh itself, and then to engage in stimulating, enjoyable activities. But most of the leisure-time activities that people participate in do not stimulate the mind, they deaden it. Instead of giving the mind the healthy exercise it needs, the mind becomes torpid and stagnant.

Think of it this way: If you want to improve your tennis game, you should always try to play against someone who plays a better game than you do. If you constantly play against people whom you can easily defeat, your game will only go downhill. When you play against a better player, you must try harder. You also have the opportunity of learning new skills from your opponent.

Each evening when you sit down in front of your T.V., you are playing against an inferior opponent. Watching too much television drains you of your energy, provides little or no challenge for your intellect, and gives you no exercise to burn off calories and eliminate your nervous energy. Don't get me wrong. I have spent many enjoyable hours roosting in front of the tube. Occasionally there are good programs on television. High-quality talk shows, dramatic productions, motion pictures, comedies, and other programs can provide you with relaxation and necessary mental stimulation. But you must learn the difference between use and abuse. The key word when it comes to television viewing, if you're really serious about overcoming stress, is *moderation*.

Two particularly stressful offerings of television are evening news programs and commercials. If you are prone to tension and stress, you should minimize your consumption of world and local news. Worrying about the latest world and national disasters is not going to ease your tensions. It is good to be informed, but it is unnecessary to be overinformed about the news. This would not be the case if the focus of the T.V. news programming was more balanced. The old adage, "No news is good news" should become a new motto for you.

Probably the most engaging, and at the same time most stressful, parts of television are commercials. You are subjected to approximately two minutes of these for every fifteen minutes of viewing time. When you watch them, you are manipulated by a variety of straight and subliminal advertising devices that cause you to buy everything from cars to panty hose. Commercials work. They are not something that you watch and forget. Their subliminal messages are registering on your unconscious mind and conditioning you to buy products you don't really need. Unfortunately, you have to pay both the economic and stress price for their effectiveness.

Consider the average commercial and how it induces stress. It will be easier for you to do this if you think like an advertiser. Imagine that you have a product that you want to sell. Since more Americans watch television than any other medium, you know that T.V. will reach the masses. Now, you have to get your message across in thirty or sixty seconds. In that amount of time, you have to convince the public that your product is worth buying. How are you going to do it? Through subliminal stimulation and by creating false expectations.

In order to reach those people out there, you must first capture their interest. Sex is still the best way, although more sophisticated subliminal techniques are occasionally employed. Start your commercial by showing your product being used by an attractive woman or man. By filling your commercial with as many erotic connotations as you legally can, you subliminally condition the viewer to associate your product with pleasurable sexual stimulation. For a full sixty seconds you stimulate the viewers in every way you can. If you do this successfully, your product is bound to sell.

Advertising is not evil. It is the best way to let people know about merchandise and services. I personally enjoy commercials; they are ingenious. Far more money and thought go into a one-minute commercial than a half-hour T.V. show. The problem is that they create false expectations within you which will never be fulfilled; they condition you to believe that happiness will come to you through your purchase.

It is important to raise the standard of our living conditions, but believing that happiness and fulfillment come exclusively through the purchase of the latest model car, or other goods and services, only paves the way for stress and tension. Do you remember the happiness and pride you felt when you purchased your first car, home, or made any other important investments? The feeling is wonderful. But how long does that feeling last? After a few days or weeks have passed, your purchase no longer thrills you. Then you begin to think in terms of acquiring something else that will again give the happiness your previous purchase temporarily afforded you. Advertising tries to perpetuate this cycle of constant purchasing. The incorrect equation that you make when you participate in this vicious behavior cycle is:

Purchasing New Goods = Happiness and Satisfaction

Don't constantly look for happiness through your purchases. Yes, raise your standard of living and get the things that you want and enjoy. But don't create false expectations for yourself by believing that the next purchase you make will bring you lasting happiness. If you do, your frustration will only add to your stress and anxiety. Realize that lasting happiness can only come from leading a balanced life and developing your physical, intellectual, and spiritual capacities. Enjoy the commodities of our technological society, but try not to find your happiness in them. Objects and possessions can't make you happy. They may add to the happiness you already possess. But by themselves they will not bring fulfillment to your life. Only you can make yourself happy.

Some Strategies for Leisure-Time Relaxation

● Beware of television and learn to use it to enhance, not ruin, your life. Don't throw your set away. There are many programs that are worthy of your attention. But don't substitute watching television for living your own life. Remember, *television will not relax you.*

● Immediately after coming home from work, take a shower and change into comfortable clothing. Then spend five minutes practicing one of the Total Relaxation Core Techniques. If you are especially tired, take a *short* nap or practice the Total Relaxation Deep Relaxation Technique given at the end of Chapter Nine.

● Instead of sitting down in front of the television set, go out and jog or walk. You will find that physical exercise will significantly diminish your tensions and rekindle your enthusiasm for living.

● Try not to eat too much immediately after returning home from work. Have something light if you are very hungry. Avoid making a habit of relaxing with an alcoholic drink each night. If you must drink, limit your drinking as much as possible. Alcohol will not relax you as much as it will depress you, particularly when you are tired.

● Force yourself to do something other than watch T.V. Read, visit friends, take an evening course. If you feel the need to escape, go out to a movie. You will get out for a while and avoid commercials.

● When you watch T.V., watch yourself as well. Observe

your level of awareness. Ask yourself if you are really gaining anything beneficial from your hours in front of the set.

● When commercials come on, watch them and observe how they have been constructed to subliminally brainwash you. Analyze them and note the types of false expectations that are being pushed upon you. If you are aware of the process, it will not affect you as much.

● Don't live the lives of the constructed characters on T.V. instead of your own life. Spend time with your family and friends instead. You'll find that your own life is much more fulfilling and relaxing than the television world.

● When you watch T.V., try to avoid the more mindless shows. Television talk shows and many of the programs on your local educational station will both entertain and stimulate you. Try to watch them instead.

The Total Relaxation Stress-Free Weekend Formula

STEP ONE: let's assume that you have Saturday and Sunday off (although the same scheme can be applied to any two-day period). On Saturday, accomplish any *necessary* errands. Do your shopping, laundry, house or yard work, and so on. That evening, make it a point to get out of the house, even if it's only for a few hours. Go out to eat, take in a movie or a play, go to a dance or party, or engage in some other leisure-time activity that you enjoy. Your Saturday night forays need not be expensive. Having dinner with friends or going to an inexpensive movie is affordable on most budgets. If you have children, hire a babysitter on Saturday night. Most babysitters are fairly inexpensive and will only cost a few dollars.

Try not to overdo it when you go out. Have a good time, but watch your consumption of food and alcohol. A third drink or an extra helping of food is really not going to make you enjoy the evening more. If you overindulge, you will only regret it the next morning.

STEP TWO in our stress-free weekend formula is to avoid planning any particular activity for Sunday. When you wake up, see how you feel. Then let the day direct itself. Don't spend the day in front of the T.V. or moping around your home. Be active and enjoy the day. Allow your spontaneous and creative interests to direct your activities. Try doing something different each Sunday. Fly a kite, go to a concert, explore a different part of your town. Make it a point to get outside for exercise if the weather is good. Avoid the Sunday newspaper doldrums. Ritual Sunday newspaper reading can be as bad as ritual T.V. watching. Let Sunday be your day to enjoy you. Spend some time by yourself. Throughout the week you are surrounded by people. Take a walk or a drive by yourself. Spend time in nature. Meditate on who you are. Consider if your life is heading in the direction that you want it to. If not, then formulate realistic plans to change it.

Sunday evening is a good time to prepare yourself for the week ahead. The coming week will hold as many challenges and opportunities as you allow it to. Make it a habit on Sunday nights to jot down on a piece of paper a few of the things you would like to accomplish during the week. Don't make your list overly complex or unrealistic. Then, the next Sunday after making your new list, look at the list you made the previous week. See how many of the things on your list you actually accomplished. If you didn't accomplish some of the items on your list, try to understand why not. Was it because you really didn't want to? Will it just take more work and time? Or were you expecting too much of yourself? After completing your list, enjoy the remainder of your evening. Remember, life is as relaxed as you make it.

Stressful Holidays

During the holiday season, which should be a time of joy and relaxation, you are subjected to a variety of stresses far different from the types of stress you are accustomed to experiencing during the rest of the year. More people commit suicide during the end of the year holiday seasons than at any other time of the year. At holiday times, there are also significant rises in the number of heart attacks and other stress-related ailments. The majority of holiday stresses are environmental ones fostered by both media and cultural conditioning.

Let us use Christmas as a representative holiday. During the Christmas season, families come together to express warmth and love for each other and for God. It is traditionally a time of joy when you are able to remove yourself from the day-to-day cares of your life and enjoy peace, fun, and companionship.

But for most people, Christmas is a nightmare of stresses, tensions, and anxieties. The premise of love and brotherhood is abrogated by the rush to buy dozens of gifts, prepare complex meals, decorate the house, mail Christmas cards, and deal with an endless stream of relatives, friends, and children who continually invade your house and leave it a shambles. For most women, the best part of Christmas is when it's all over. Instead of looking forward to Christmas, they see it as an inevitable hassle at the end of each year.

What happened to Christmas? Its true meaning has been lost under a welter of tinsel, blinking Christmas-tree lights, unnecessary presents and food, long lines at department stores, longer lines at exchange counters, not enough money to buy everyone the presents they want, and the all-pervasive feeling that you have either forgotten something important or that you just didn't do a good enough job.

No wonder most women get the Christmas blues. They spend weeks planning and preparing. Then the family arrives at home, Christmas dinner is consumed in a matter of hours, the presents are unwrapped, and everyone goes off in his or her own direction, leaving Mom sitting alone staring at the tree, looking at the presents that have been given to her, wondering resentfully if it was all really worthwhile.

Most women are caught in a trap. They have to go through the senseless rituals of Christmas commercialism because they believe that everyone will be disappointed if they don't. Mom will work herself to death to please everyone she loves. Then, suddenly, it's all over. Through her exhaustion an overwhelming feeling of alienation and loneliness will begin to fill her. This is the time when many women commit suicide or have a nervous collapse.

Mom's problem is compounded by the fact that everyone else seems to be having such a wonderful time. The kids and relatives all seem happy, Dad is preoccupied with a football game on T.V., yet Mom feels alone, empty, and exhausted. She assumes that there must be something desperately wrong with her.

Gift-Giving Stress

The majority of holiday stresses occur because the atmosphere of the holiday season is based upon consumerism.

Money = Happiness.
The More Expensive the Present = The More I Love You.

This concept is pushed upon us by our commercial society. All of the advertisements you encounter during the holidays reinforce the idea that if you really love someone, you will give him an expensive gift. This is absurd. Loving someone does not necessarily involve the giving of material presents. Loving someone means loving someone. Did that extra necktie, electric shoeshine machine, food processor, or cookbook really express the true quality of your love? Probably not.

Think of the stress created by the assumption that people will be disappointed if you don't get them the "right" gift. You stand, along with millions of other tense and nervous persons, in long lines to buy gifts that people really don't want or need. You experience additional stress because you probably don't have enough money to buy the gifts you would really prefer. So you either have to shell out more money, which will make you tense because you can't really afford it, or buy less expensive gifts and experience stress brought on by guilt. You're stuck in the "damned if you do, and guilty if you don't" trap.

It is also absurd to believe that holidays will make up for all the wrong things we have done to each other all year. The classic example of this is the man who cheats on his wife and then, after fully enjoying himself, buys her flowers or takes her out to dinner to "make up" for his behavior. If he really had felt so badly about what he was doing, he wouldn't have done it in the first place. If he had done something he was sorry for, the best thing would not have been to "say it with flowers," but simply not to repeat the same wrong action.

It is not a new observation that during the holiday season people treat each other the way they should all year long. After a year of abusing each other, most people try and assuage their guilt by giving to each other. It is certainly a wonderful idea to give gifts to each other out of love. But to give gifts out of guilt or because it is "traditional" only promotes unnecessary stress.

One of the easiest ways to overcome tension and frustration is to give of yourself. Giving of yourself does not necessitate spending hundreds of dollars or slaving away in the kitchen for untold hours. Self giving means that you care enough for someone to spend your time with him or her. You are willingly giving her the gift of yourself.

All of the presents in the world will not overcome any abuse to another human being. An iota of love will. If the presents that you give are really an expression of your love, it doesn't matter how expensive or fancy they are. Your present is the emblem of your love, it is a material symbol that you care for someone. But your presents do not buy love, nor are they love.

The easiest and simplest way to avoid holiday stress is to view the holidays as a time to love and be loved. When you sit around the holiday tree or dinner table, don't measure your success in the number of presents you have given or received, or in whether the turkey or roast is cooked well. Measure your success in your ability to love and to gratefully accept the love of those around you.

Don't expect any thanks or gratitude for your efforts. If you do, you will be paving the way for disappointment and stress. Concern yourself with giving, not with receiving. But don't let your giving be compelled by guilt, by a false equation between money and love, or by convention. Let your giving be governed by your love. If you apply this principle, and employ the following strategies, you will find that the holidays can be a time of true joy, love, peace, and relaxation.

Strategies for Overcoming Holiday Stress

● Be sensitive to the needs of others during the holiday season, but don't overlook your own needs. If you expend all your energy preparing for the holidays and are exhausted when they finally arrive, you have done too much. Reconsider the types of meals you plan, the amount of entertaining that you do, and the types of presents that you purchase. See if you can simplify all of these things to some degree.

● If cooking is too much of a bother, try eating out. Invite your relatives and friends over and have a buffet. Request that each one of them bring a different food, making sure that you oversee what they bring so that you don't end up with twelve plates of potato salad.

● Consider the role of the homemaker. Whoever is in charge of the cooking, household, and gift preparations receives the largest part of the holiday stress. Be aware of the strain he or she is under. Try to help as much as possible.

● Don't feel that holidays are a chore which you are forced to go through each year. If you do, you are only conditioning yourself for tension. Try to see holidays in a new light. Concentrate less on outer preparations and more on love and family unity. If you are tense, depressed, or fatigued from overwork, the holidays can lose all their joy both for you and for the people you love.

● Learn to avoid the long lines in stores, either by shopping early or by avoiding the larger department and chain stores. Many of the smaller stores have more interesting and less expensive gifts, and their environment and service is usually more casual and relaxed.

● Try giving non-traditional gifts. Instead of spending large sums of money on gifts which will be worn or used once or twice and then forgotten, give presents that are either more utilitarian, or simply fun. If time allows, and you enjoy the process, it can be very satisfying to make gifts. Some sample non-traditional gift ideas are: Go to a greenhouse and buy everyone on your list a plant. A plant is a living gift that will provide beauty and joy throughout the year. Make cookies or bake something for a present. Give someone tickets to a movie or a play. Give someone a gift subscription to *National Geographic, Audubon,* or some other magazine. This is a fairly inexpensive gift that arrives throughout the year and is an ever-present reminder of your love. These are just a few sample ideas. You can probably use your own creative imagination to come up with even better ones. The point is not to think in terms of "having" to buy someone an expensive present, but "wanting" to buy a unique present.

● Don't try to make up for your past behavior during the holidays. A new sweater or camera is no substitute for love. If you want to give someone a real gift, then give him a new and improved you. Stop hurting and start loving each other. Don't put off your reconciliation with someone you love for another time. Life may not give you another holiday together. Do and be everything you want . . . NOW. Holidays are special times when you express your affection outwardly. Don't lose this spirit throughout the year. Every day is a holiday if you see it in the right light.

● Talk to the other members of your family and ask them what changes they would like to make in the way you celebrate the holidays. Invent some traditions just for your family. Sing songs together, do a group reading of the *Journey of the Magi* or other religious or traditional verses, watch or read Dickens's *A Christmas Carol* together. And when it's all over, don't allow yourself to get the "after-the-holidays blues." As soon as the holidays are over, start a new project that interests you. Don't sit around and wait for depression to find you. Be active. It's hard to hit a moving target, so keep moving.

● Don't expect those around you to please you in the way that you want to be pleased. When your expectations are unfulfilled, you will only be tense and frustrated. Let everyone please you in his or her own way. True peace of mind will come only when you enjoy others as they are, without placing your expectations upon them.

● Above all, when you are with your family and friends during the holiday season, enjoy them. Remember that the shortcut to overcoming holiday stress is to be more concerned with giving than receiving. Be concerned with giving love, harmony, peace, and relaxation, and be less concerned with material presents, foods, and other preparations. Then your holidays will be real holidays for all.

Special Problems

The sound of a supersonic airplane, standing in a line while waiting for a bank teller, sitting in your car at the toll plaza, waiting to buy or exchange an item, the sound of your boss's voice, or any other form of stress that comes from *outside of yourself* can easily upset you, trigger your fight or flight response, and result in damage to your mind and body.

You will find that Total Relaxation Core Technique #4, The Sphere of Power, will enable you to negate the effects of even the most powerful environmental stresses. This technique will *immediately* allow you to take control of yourself and stop the deleterious effects of environmental stress.

TOTAL RELAXATION TECHNIQUE #4

THE SPHERE OF POWER

Practice this Total Relaxation exercise whenever you feel tension entering into you from outside. This exercise can be practiced while you work, talk with others, drive a car, or engage in any activity. This exercise is particularly effective when you need to stop tension, frustration, or panic immediately.

Focus your attention upon the center of your stomach, in the area of your navel. Feel that this is an area of tremendous strength. Visualize a clear sphere, a dome of energy surrounding your entire body, which is supported by your own willpower. Positive thoughts, feelings, ideas, and vibrations can pass through this sphere and reach you. But as long as you visualize this sphere of clear energy surrounding you, negative thoughts, hostilities, anger, and aggressive feelings of other persons and situations cannot enter you.

While you imagine this sphere of clear energy surrounding you, feel that you are consciously directing energy from the center of your body, in the area of your navel, throughout the sphere. Feel that the energy of your willpower can easily deflect tension-causing feelings and frustrations that are directed inside you from the outside world. You will find that with repeated practice it becomes easier and easier to visualize this sphere of energy, and that you will be able to stop the negative energy of others from entering you.

Five

The Relaxation Diet

Reason directs the mind.
Love feeds the heart.
—SRI CHINMOY

There is a direct and important correlation between the amount and types of foods you eat and your susceptibility to stress. If you have a well-balanced diet that is particularly high in the B-complex vitamins, you will be less susceptible to environmental and other forms of stress. However, if you have a poor diet, or if you undereat or overeat, you are a prime candidate for high blood pressure, stroke, heart disease, and many other stress-related ailments.

Recent government studies have confirmed what many food and nutrition experts have been saying for years: Americans are one of the most overfed and undernourished peoples in the world. This seemingly incongruous situation has occurred because of the public's lack of knowledge about what constitutes good nutrition, and because many of the less nutritious "fast foods" have been extensively advertised, causing an increase in their consumption and a proportionate decrease in the consumption of more nutritious foods.

Your body requires five basic types of nutrients: proteins, minerals, vitamins, carbohydrates, and fats. If your body does not get a sufficient amount of any of these types of nutrients, then it will be more susceptible to stress. The quantity of nutrients you require will vary according to the types of mental and physical activity you are engaged in, and also according to the amount of stress you are subjected to.

Food: You Are What You Eat

We live in a society where we are constantly exposed to food. We use food in our social and business activities, as a method of rewarding ourselves, as an expression of love, as an escape from stress and worry, and as a means of enjoyment. With all the emphasis we place on food, it is no wonder that over half of the men and women in the United States are overweight.

If you are overweight, you are more susceptible to stress and high blood pressure. Approximately fifty percent of all obese people suffer from high blood pressure. In most cases, obesity is simply the result of overeating. However, in some cases it can be the result of glandular or other physiological disorders.

Stress from being overweight occurs for two principal reasons. When you are overweight, your heart has to work harder to supply your additional fatty tissues with blood, oxygen, and nutrients. The constant strain on your heart can result in high blood pressure, exhaustion, fatigue, and heart disease. Secondly, you may incur a great deal of stress because of your appearance, your inability to lose weight, or other physical or psychological limitations that excess weight places upon you. Worrying about being overweight may only cause you to eat more. It's a vicious cycle: *The more you eat → The more you worry about your weight and appearance → The more you eat.*

While some people tend to react to stress by overeating, others react by eating too little. Stress often results in painful stomach cramps, making it difficult for an individual to eat enough. Prolonged stress can induce nausea and vomiting, preventing you from assimilating food.

If you are underweight, you are probably depriving your body of some of the basic nutrients it needs to cope effectively with tension and stress. While it is unlikely that being underweight will raise the level of your blood pressure, poor nutrition will make you more susceptible to stress and other diseases. Being underweight can also cause you to worry about your appearance and to have trouble sleeping. Severe cases of stress occasionally result in anorexia nervosa, a mental condition that causes a person to become obsessed with dieting and weight loss, which can ultimately lead to death from starvation.

Meat

Meat is expensive and hard to digest. Most physicians agree that the vast majority of Americans eat too much meat. Meat contains large amounts of cholesterol and uric acid, both of which can be harmful to your body. While the cholesterol question is still being debated in the halls of science, it is a good idea, pending further results, to try to avoid fatty meats.

Studies have shown that people who have significantly reduced the amount of meat that they eat, or who follow a vegetarian diet, are less susceptible to the negative effects of stress than persons who eat larger quantities of meat.

Meat can also be unhealthy due to the way animals are raised. To increase profits, most animals are raised in enclosed stockyards, or factory farms where they are confined and overcrowded until they are slaughtered. Normally, overcrowding causes outbreaks of disease, resulting in the death of many of the animals. In order to prevent this and to combat parasites, stockyard animals are given large doses of antibiotics. Many of these chemicals (including hormones, which are used to increase the weight and size of an animal) are retained in the animals' fatty tissues and passed directly to you. Furthermore, many meats are dyed in order to make them more attractive to the customer in the market. Some of these artificial dyes are known carcinogens and have been directly linked to cancer of the breast, bladder, stomach, and colon.

The Negative Effects of
Stimulants and Depressants

Both the level of your blood pressure and your susceptibility to stress are exacerbated by stimulants. Caffeine, theophylline, theobromine, and maté (substances contained in coffee, tea, cola, and chocolate) overstimulate your nervous system and cause an unnatural rise in the level of your metabolism. The result is tension, fatigue, nervousness, insomnia, headaches, mild paranoia, and depression.

Caffeine and similar chemicals are highly addictive drugs which can create both physiological and psychological dependencies. If you are a regular coffee or tea drinker, you may be caught up in the addiction-stress cycle:

Drug-induced stress →	*Drug-induced relief* →	*Drug-induced stress*
I feel nervous and tense because my body needs coffee.	I feel relaxed now that I have had a cup of coffee and I have temporarily assuaged my addiction.	I feel nervous and tense because my body requires a cup of coffee again.

When you are addicted to stimulating drugs, you feel tense and stressful every time your body needs to fulfill its addiction. When your body's need has been met, you will have a temporary sense of relief. But this feeling of relief will only last until your body again requires the drug. Until you have fulfilled its need, you will experience stress and tension.

Tobacco

Smoking has been linked to heart disease, lung cancer, and other dangerous diseases. The incidence of stroke in people who have high blood pressure and who smoke is over ten times higher than in people who have high blood pressure and don't smoke. Smoking is especially dangerous for people who have arteriosclerosis. Nicotine causes their partially clogged blood vessels to constrict, making it even harder for blood to flow, and greatly increasing the chances of heart attack and stroke. Like caffeine, nicotine is a highly addictive drug. Regular use of it will also cause you to become caught up in the addiction-stress cycle.

Alcohol

While an occasional drink may give you a mild feeling of relaxation, steady or heavy drinking causes you to experience more, not less stress. Unlike caffeine and nicotine, which are stimulants, alcohol is a depressant and will make you feel tired, down, and generally unfulfilled. Alcohol depletes your body of its B-complex vitamins, which are essential for resistance to stress. It is highly addictive, creating stress through both psychological and physiological dependency. Consuming large quantities of alcoholic beverages can also result in permanent damage to the liver and other essential organs of the body.

The Relaxation Diet*

The Relaxation Diet is a stress-free approach to eating. It is composed of a variety of strategies and suggestions which, when effectively implemented, will significantly reduce stress. Choose those strategies which seem applicable to your particular needs and gradually introduce them into your lifestyle. Do not expect to change your eating habits overnight. Beneficial and lasting changes in diet occur gradually.

Part One—Types of Foods

● Try to follow a balanced diet. If you are unsure as to what constitutes a balanced diet, ask your doctor to recommend some literature on the subject.

● It is generally a good practice to take a multiple vitamin tablet every day. Try to select a vitamin supplement that is particularly high in B-complex vitamins. However, avoid the

---

*Implement the Relaxation Diet only with the advice of your doctor.

tendency to take more vitamins than you need. It is not necessary for you to take a multiple vitamin and two or three additional "stress formula" vitamin supplements. One high-potency multiple vitamin will probably fill all of your vitamin needs, unless you have a particular vitamin deficiency.

• Taking too many or the wrong kinds of vitamins can make you nervous and tense. A prime example of this is the abuse of Vitamin E. Vitamin E and other fat-soluble vitamins (A, D, and K) are retained in your tissues and have a tendency to build up to toxic levels. If you are unsure about what kinds of vitamins or what dosages you should take, consult your physician or a licensed dietician.

• Try to eliminate or minimize your consumption of white sugar, and of products such as candy, donuts, and presweetened cereals that contain high concentrations of sugar. Sugar tends to make people hyperactive by overstimulating their metabolism. Following this overstimulation, many people experience a mild depression known as the "sugar blues." Refined sugar destroys B-complex vitamins and has been linked to a variety of other diseases. If you use sugar in moderation, you can still enjoy it while avoiding its harmful effects.

• Try to minimize your intake of salt, especially if you are prone to hypertension. Studies have shown that salt often raises the blood pressure of people who are prone to hypertension. Both sugar and salt are found in such a wide variety of food products that it is virtually impossible to eliminate them from your diet. But avoiding products that contain large amounts of sugar and salt will help you to stay relaxed and avoid high blood pressure.

• Try to avoid greasy and oily foods. They tend to upse your stomach and the resulting discomfort can easily aggravate a nervous condition.

• Try to minimize your consumption of coffee, tea, cola,

chocolate, and other products that contain caffeine, theophylline, theobromine, and other stimulants. It is not necessary to eliminate these foods totally from your diet. If you use them occasionally they will not harm you, but frequent use will become abuse, and you will suffer the consequences of the addiction-stress cycle.

● Instead of drinking coffee, try Sanka or herbal teas. Give yourself a week or two to adjust to the change in flavor. You may find that the new freeze-dried decaffeinated coffees taste just as good as the original.

● Don't be fooled by colas and diet sodas. Often these products contain more caffeine than a cup of strong coffee.

● Instead of eating three big meals each day, try eating one substantial meal and two smaller meals.

● Eat as many fresh fruits and vegetables as you can. They are an excellent and natural source of B-complex and other vitamins.

● Try to avoid boredom in your meals by varying the types of foods and the times at which you eat. A fixed mealtime or eating the same foods on specific days because it is "convenient" or because you are "used to it" can create unnecessary stress through boredom. Don't fear the unknown. Try new foods! Pick up a new cookbook and experiment. Eat out more often. Vary your routines. You will be more relaxed and gain more joy if you do.

Part Two—A Relaxed Approach to Eating

In order to gain the most benefit and enjoyment from your food, it is necessary to relax while eating. If you are nervous and tense before or during a meal, then you will decrease the effectiveness of your digestive system. Mealtime should be a time for you to forget about your problems and difficulties.

● Try to avoid eating too fast. While you are eating, occasionally take short breaks. Put your food aside and look around you for a minute. Take a breath and relax. Then resume eating slowly. Repeat this several times during each meal.

● If you are in a state of severe stress, don't eat. Wait until you have relaxed. Instead of eating when you are tense, practice one of the Total Relaxation Core Techniques for a few minutes until you have dissipated your tension. Then, in a calm and relaxed state of mind, enjoy your meal.

● When you eat with others, avoid discussing topics that may make you or the people you are with tense. Discuss topics of mutual interest that promote agreement and good feelings for all who are present.

● Try to avoid reading or watching T.V. while you are eating. Instead, pay more attention to your food. If you try to do two things at once, the chances are that you will not do either of them well. Give your full attention to your food and then give your full attention to your book, newspaper, or whatever else may interest you.

● When the weather is favorable, eat outside. Have your lunch in the park or cook dinner on your patio for a change of pace.

● Try to avoid crowded restaurants. It is very hard to be relaxed while eating when surrounded by dozens of other people. Try taking your lunch hour a little earlier or later than you normally do. You'll avoid the crowds and get better service, too.

● When eating out, don't become upset if the service is slow. You can either wait or leave. But getting upset is not going to make the cook prepare your food any faster. Instead of getting upset, content yourself with waiting. Enjoy the people you are with, read something, or just daydream for a few minutes.

● If the food in a restaurant is not satisfactory, don't get upset. Send it back and order something different. Or you can simply feel that you can't always expect to get the most delicious food at every meal and content yourself with what you have received.

● Avoid fast food restaurants whenever possible. If you are in such a rush that you can't take more than a minute or two to eat, then don't eat. Have something to drink or a snack and postpone eating until you have more time.

● Never hurry through a meal. Let the world wait for a few minutes; it will survive.

● Avoid eating while driving. Not only is it a stressful habit, but it could be dangerous. Pull over for a minute and enjoy your food. Then resume driving.

● Try to avoid overeating. It will only cause you to feel tired and uncomfortable. Enjoy eating moderately. You will place your body under less stress if you do.

Part Three—Losing Weight

If you are overweight, you are constantly placing a strain on your heart and other internal organs. When you are overweight, you get tired more quickly and are not as happy with the way you look. It's amazing what losing a few pounds can do for your outlook on life and your self-image. But the eternal question is: how do you lose weight?

If you feel that it is important to lose weight, then you must actively consider how to avoid gaining weight. For most people, losing weight is not the problem, it's keeping weight off that creates the most difficulties. There are hundreds of good diet books on the market that can show you how to lose your extra pounds. But very few of them can show you how to stay thin.

The best way to reach your proper weight is to stop worrying about it. Worrying will not make those extra pounds disappear. Worry will only make you upset, nervous, and tense. Instead, try some of the following strategies:

● Drink two full glasses of water before every meal. You

will find that you will eat much less if you drink water before, instead of during, your meals.

● Fast, or only eat a small quantity of food on the first day of your diet. After the first day, only eat when you are hungry. Your body will tell you when to eat and when not to eat. Overweight persons eat out of boredom, because they are tense, or simply because they like the taste of food. But if you only eat when you are hungry, you will quickly attain your proper weight.

● Don't feel that you are going on a diet. If you do, you will automatically assume that it will only be a *temporary* change in your normal eating habits. Instead, feel that you are going to change your eating habits for life. This change will be neither radical nor boring. You will simply eat less of the types of foods that you eat now, and you will avoid a few foods which are too fattening.

● Avoid crash diets, protein diets, and prolonged fasting unless you are under the strict supervision of a physician. Following these types of diets often subjects both your mind and body to unnecessary and dangerous amounts of stress.

● Remember that eating does not bring happiness. On the contrary, overeating creates physical and psychological stress. Before eating, always ask yourself: "Is this something I really want to eat? Am I eating out of need, or am I just eating out of boredom, nervousness, or because I am with other people who are eating?

● Get enough exercise. If you exercise regularly, you will burn off unwanted calories and you will generally become more conscious of your physical appearance. Abdominal and stomach exercises are good for helping you lose weight and for keeping weight off. When your stomach muscles are in good shape, you won't want to eat as much because you will feel "full" sooner.

● Be honest with yourself. You know if you are overweight or not. Wearing a larger size pair of pants or dress may fool others, but it won't fool you. If you have a weight problem, then do something about it today. From this moment on, resolve to change your eating habits. Start now. If you plan to start your diet "tomorrow," then you probably never will. Start right this second. And if you break your diet, don't waste time feeling bad or guilty about it; simply get right back on the diet.

● Learn to listen to your body. Your body is an incredibly sophisticated organic machine which is the product of millions of years of evolution. It will always tell you exactly what you need and don't need to eat. Following rigid or standardized diets may be dangerous because you may need more of one type of nutrient than someone else does. If you eat the foods that your body tells you to, you will have a balanced and moderate diet.

● Avoid junk foods. You can allow yourself occasional sweets, but don't overindulge.

● Stop eating when you feel full. Your parents may have told you to always eat everything on your plate. This might have been good for you when you were nine or ten years old, constantly active, and if your plate was not too full. But it is no longer necessary.

● Make it a habit to have smaller portions. Don't be as concerned with banning specific foods from your diet as with eating smaller amounts of them. If you buy an ice cream cone, ask for one scoop instead of your normal two By following this practice with everything you eat, you will not be overweight.

● Keep an adequate supply of non-fattening food on hand, such as apples, melba toast, grapefruits, diet and vegetable juice drinks, and yogurt. Try to avoid keeping too many highly caloric foods around. It is much easier to resist temptation if temptation is not staring you in the face.

● If you go on an eating binge, don't get depressed, because you'll probably only eat more. If you overeat, then resolve more firmly to stick to your diet. But don't make the same mistake twice.

● Avoid going for long periods of time without eating. If you do, you will become so hungry that when you finally eat you will overeat. Eat moderately several times a day instead.

● It is important to have a good breakfast, but not necessarily a big breakfast. Ignore cereal company propaganda and try to cut down your morning intake.

Part Four—Gaining Weight

If you are underweight because of nervousness or stress, then try employing the following strategies:

● Become more conscious of food. Don't think of eating as a chore, but as an enjoyable and natural experience.

● When you eat, try to eat in pleasant surroundings either by yourself or with people you like.

● Practice a Total Relaxation Core Technique before eating. You will find that food is much more appealing when you are relaxed.

● Make sure that you get enough exercise and fresh air. Regular exercise will stimulate your appetite naturally.

● At times, you may have to force yourself to eat. If this is necessary, then it is better to eat small quantities of food more frequently. By forcing yourself to eat large amounts of food, you will only condition yourself to dislike it.

● Consult a physician about diet supplements. If you are underweight, chances are that you may be lacking some essential vitamins, proteins, or other nutrients. If you only eat small quantities of food, you should be more conscious of its quality. Check with your doctor to see if he has any special recommendations.

THE ROSE

Visualize a beautiful rose in the center of your chest. It is not necessary, when doing this exercise, to see a clear picture of the rose. Simply do the best you can to imagine a soft, reddish rose in the center of your chest. If other thoughts and images pass through your mind while you're performing this exercise, simply ignore them.

Imagine that the rose is completely folded up; none of the petals has unfolded. Now, as you focus your attention upon the reddish rose in the center of your chest, imagine that the first set of petals, the outer row of petals, are gradually unfolding. As they do so, imagine them growing and expanding and filling the entire area of your chest. Simultaneously feel that a wave of peace and joy is spreading throughout your entire chest area. Then imagine that a second set of rose petals is unfolding. Slowly and gently they unfold and expand, this time filling the entire area of your body. And again, feel another wave of peace and joy, even deeper than the first, starting in the center of the chest, in the center of the rose, and expanding outwards, filling your entire body with peace and joy. Now visualize a third set of petals, again starting in the center of the rose, and imagine them expanding outwards, filling up the entire room, spreading peace and joy everywhere throughout the room or area in which you are located. Then visualize a fourth set of petals opening up, this time expanding and filling the entire earth. Feel that peace and joy are spreading from the center of your chest, from the center of the rose, throughout all of the earth, and filling all of the people, all of the beings and all of the objects on this earth with peace and joy. Now visualize another set of petals opening up, this time filling the entire solar system. And simultaneously feel that you are spreading your own inner peace, of which you have an infinite supply, through-out the entire solar system. Then visualize that a seventh row of petals is opening up, this time filling up the entire universe, spreading peace and joy throughout the universe and into the infinite.

As you practice this exercise, continue to imagine additional petals of the rose unfolding. As each set of petals unfolds, and spreads out into the infinite, feel that they are reaching further and further out and spreading a deeper peace and joy throughout your whole being, throughout all of existence. There is no end to the petals of the inner rose. Continue to unfold set after set of petals for as long as you wish to practice this exercise. As you do so, you will find yourself constantly entering deeper and deeper into a state of total relaxation.

Six

Exercise To Relax

A proper amount of exercise is essential for overcoming worry, stress, tension, and fatigue because it dissipates your nervous energy before you internalize it. If you do not get at least twenty minutes of vigorous physical activity each day, it is extremely difficult to overcome the negative effects of stress. Regardless of your age or the state of your health, it is essential that you exercise regularly each day.

When you exercise you strengthen your physical body and gain higher resistance to environmental and psychological stress. And, when done in the correct frame of mind, exercise will also help to distract you from your problems, worries, and anxieties. In this sense, exercise is relaxation. While your body exercises, your mind relaxes.

The Total Relaxation approach to exercise can be summed up in one word, *moderation*. If you wish to eliminate stress and tension from your body and mind, it is essential that you exercise regularly four or five days a week. When selecting the form of exercise that will be best for you, take into consideration your own particular strengths and weaknesses. Then work on developing a noncompetitive attitude toward athletics by employing the advice and strategies presented in this chapter. Otherwise, your exercise program will only increase, rather than decrease, your tension.

It is essential to assess the state of your health before you begin any exercise program. If you are over forty, it would be a good idea to have a treadmill-electrocardiogram—stress test—to determine the strength of your heart. Your doctor will interpret the results and advise you as to what types of exercise are right for you. If you have had a heart attack, knee injury, or any other physical problem that has affected your physical health, you must view exercising in a different light than a healthy eighteen-year-old would.

If you are a world class athlete, then exercise is your business and you have evolved safe and sensible training schedules for working out. However, if you are a weekend athlete, or you do not consider yourself to be particularly athletic, you must be very careful about both your approach and attitude towards exercise.

If you are over thirty, you should realize that your body can no longer do some of the things it could when you were younger. While you may still "feel" the same, your body is not the same. If you approach exercise as something *to succeed at* instead of something that will benefit you, then exercise can harm you. You must become aware of your physical limitations and form a positive psychological approach towards exercise.

Most people incur problems with exercise because they have the wrong attitude. They feel that exercise is always competitive. If they are out jogging and someone runs past them, they feel slighted. Whenever they play tennis, golf, handball, or any other sport, their primary goal is to triumph over their opponent. Their entire game is directed towards one goal: Conquest. If they win, they achieve the "thrill of victory." If they lose, they experience the "agony of defeat." While this attitude might possibly improve their chances of winning, it also causes them to be filled with worry, stress, and tension.

As a boy, Will Lewis was an avid sports enthusiast. He played baseball, football, basketball, and did calisthenics on a regular basis. While he was never on the first string teams in high school or at college, he always actively participated in intramurals and small team competitions.

After Will graduated from college he took a job with a large insurance firm. He bought a new car and after several years on the job made a down-payment on a small condominium. Things were going well for him. His only complaint was that he couldn't find enough time to exercise because his job was so demanding. On the job he was either sitting at a desk or driving his car to see a client. The only exercise he received was walking from his office to his car, or from his car to a client's house.

After several years had gone by, Will began to develop a flabby stomach. He was not eating any more than when he was younger, but because he was getting less exercise and, owing to the slowing of metabolism which occurs to everyone as he grows older, eating the same quantity of food caused him to gain more and more weight.

Will decided that he needed to do something about the gradual deterioration of his body. He tried eating somewhat less. This stopped him from gaining any further weight, but it didn't help him to lose weight. He decided to join the Y.M.C.A., feeling that exercise was the key element that was missing in his weight loss program.

But before Will started his exercise program, he started to encounter problems on his job. He was a commissioned salesman and was dependent upon new business for the bulk of his salary. But, owing to a minor recession, people weren't buying as much insurance as they had been for the preceding few years and Will suddenly found himself without enough money to pay his mortgage and other bills.

Will had to give up his projected exercise program so that he could put in more time on his job. He was under tremendous financial pressure and needed exercise more than ever to help him release some of his tensions. But he simply didn't have the time, and when he did have some free time, he was so exhausted from the stress and tension he encountered on the job that he didn't feel like exercising.

One fateful Saturday afternoon, Will decided that he had had enough. He went down to the local park and played basketball for several hours with some other men who played there regularly. After an initial period of clumsiness, Will began to play well, and after a few hours, he thought his old touch was coming back. Then, unexpectedly, Will found himself lying on the ground overcome with chest pains. He was rushed to the hospital and placed in the intensive care unit. At the age of thirty-two, Will had suffered a massive heart attack. He remained in the hospital for several weeks, after which he was allowed to return home.

Walking

For most people, walking is the safest and most accessible form of exercise. It requires no special equipment or facilities and, provided you walk on relatively flat surfaces, it will place no undue strain upon your heart. Walking is recommended by more doctors for heart patients than any other form of exercise. If you can walk at a moderate pace for twenty to thirty minutes a day, you will significantly reduce the chances of having a heart attack.

Walking is also the best form of exercise for persons who are under constant pressure and stress. If you are an over-stressed individual, chances are that you will try to "work off" your stress when you exercise. However, in doing so, you will only incur more stress because you are trying too hard. One of the reasons that you are under pressure to begin with is because you probably take too aggressive an attitude when dealing with problems and difficulties in your life. When you transfer this same aggressive approach to exercise, you only incur more tension.

But walking will not permit you to be aggressive. Try it and see. If, when you walk, you feel impatient and find it boring, then keep walking. This is a sure sign that you have found the right form of exercise. Your boredom with walking is simply a manifestation of your own inner tension. You may want more mental and physical stimulation, but what you really need is to slow yourself down and enjoy life. Taking brisk walks every day will dissipate your tensions and provide you with safe and enjoyable exercise.

When you walk, or perform any exercise, it is particularly helpful if you can set specific daily hours for this activity. This will enable you to exercise more regularly. Most people find that it is easiest to exercise either immediately before or after work. If you need more joy in your life, walk in the morning. You will feel the joy that is present at the beginning of each new day. If you need more peace in your life, walk in the early evening. You will feel the peace that is present at the end of each day.

Weather is no barrier to the determined walker. When you first start walking, you may be put off by rain, cold weather, or heat. But after you have grown accustomed to taking daily walks, you will find that changes in weather lend variety to your walks.

Walking for Relaxation—Strategies

● Set a fixed time for your daily walks. Experiment to see which time is best for you. You may want to alter your walking time with the changes of the season or the changes in your business or social activities. But try to set up a realistic schedule and stick to it.

● If you live in the city, you must be concerned about the safety of where you walk. If you are worried about being mugged while you are walking, you will find it difficult to relax. You can avoid this by walking in good neighborhoods in daylight, or by walking in well-travelled areas of your city's parks. It is also a good idea to carry a tin whistle if you walk in an area where many dogs roam loose. If a dog bothers you, a good loud blow on your whistle will probably cause him to run away. If you are really terrified of dogs, carry a small can of mace, which will discourage even a trained attack dog, but it can cause damage to the eyes and should only be used as a last resort. I personally never carry anything but a few dog biscuits. I find that it is less stressful to make friends with a dog than to try to scare him away.

● Try walking with a friend. Many husbands and wives find that taking daily walks together has been beneficial both to their health and their relationship.

● When you walk, forget about your worries. Look around you and enjoy what you see. All of life is on display just for you to enjoy. If you are walking in the country, then enjoy the diversity of the trees and flowers. It can be fun to pick up a guidebook to trees, flowers, or birds and learn to identify the ones you encounter in your daily sauntering. When you walk in the city, observe the varying styles of architecture and the people around you. See if you can pick out the people who are the most tense or the most relaxed by the way they walk. Compare yourself to them. Are you more relaxed? The chances are good that you are far more relaxed because you are consciously trying.

● Enjoy the world around you when you walk. It is just as easy to see beauty in anything as it is to see ugliness. Try and see beauty. You'll be happier and more relaxed if you do.

● Vary your walk. Don't take the same old route every day. Explore new roads or blocks and see what they have to offer.

● Instead of eating a heavy lunch in a restaurant or cafeteria, have an apple and go for a walk. You will return to work feeling much more relaxed after half an hour than you will after sitting in a crowded, smoke-filled restaurant.

● Don't overdo it. When you first start your walking program, be content to walk for ten minutes. Gradually increase the time to twenty minutes or a half hour.

● When you come home from work, if you feel that you are too tired to go for a walk, go anyway. You'll find that you will be refreshed and renewed afterward and that you will get rid of the tensions you have built up during the day. Sitting in your living room, having a drink, or watching T.V. will only make you more fatigued and will not eliminate your stress.

● If you enjoy your daily walks and find that they are beneficial, then try a weekend hike. Go to a state or national park and explore the nature trails. This will give you a chance to regain your perspective by temporarily removing you from your environment. Also, you will be able to relax and enjoy the beauty of nature and the peace of the woods. Nature is never tense. Walk through the woods in any season and listen ... feel the peace and stillness. Occasional trips away from home to a relaxing environment are an excellent way to overcome tension and stress.

Other Forms of Non-Competitive Exercise

Though walking is the best method of exercise for overcoming stress, there are a number of others. However, they make more demands upon your body, and if you are unsure whether you can safely participate in them, you should consult your doctor first.

The best active forms of exercise for reducing stress and tension are jogging, swimming, and bicycling. While none of these will significantly raise the level of your blood pressure, it is still a good idea to approach them carefully.

Jogging

Jogging is one of the finest forms of exercise for overcoming tension and putting your body into top shape. But there is a great deal of difference between jogging for relaxation and running for improving your endurance. When you jog to relax, it is best to move at a slow and even pace. You are not running against a clock. You are jogging simply for the pure joy of jogging. You should not jog or run so fast that you cannot breathe comfortably. The best test to see if you are running too fast is to hum or sing now and then while you jog, or jog with someone else and have a conversation. If you find that you can't comfortably hum or converse and jog at the same time, then you are going too fast. Slow down! Enjoy the scenery as it goes by. Apply the strategies for walking to your jogging. The only difference between jogging and walking for relaxation should be the pace. Your attitude should be the same.

Bicycling for Relaxation

The advent of the ten-speed bicycle has brought bicycle riding into the province of relaxation. Formerly, it was not considered to be a particularly good form of exercise for hypertensive individuals because the effort involved in pedaling a heavy bicycle was too excessive. But the new breed of ten-speed bicycles are significantly lighter and their variety of gears makes them easier to use.

Bicycling will provide you with a wider range for exploration than walking or jogging will. Try to cycle in an area that is not filled with cars. Ride on quiet roads or on bicycle paths in your park. When you come to a hill or steep grade, instead of forcing yourself to pedal up it, hop off your bike and walk it up the hill.

If you or a friend have a car, purchase a bike rack and take your bikes with you on an adventure. Visit the shore or go to another town. The best way to see a new place is either by walking or by bicycling. Your bicycle will provide you with greater mobility and is an excellent non-competitive form of exercise.

Swimming

Swimming has often been called the perfect exercise because it is probably the only form of physical culture in which you use every muscle in your body. Non-competitive swimming is a great way to relax and burn calories at the same time. The only drawback to swimming may be your distance from a pool or to a suitable body of water.

If you swim laps in a pool, it is a good idea to change strokes every five or six laps. Most people tend to push themselves harder the longer they swim. By changing strokes every few laps, you will remind yourself that you are swimming to relax. It is also a good idea to rest or float every few laps in order to catch your breath. Don't try to conquer the pool. Enjoy it. If you are always pushing yourself to see how many laps you can swim in a short time, you will be losing the relaxing effect that swimming can have upon you. Swim for enjoyment. Your chances of swimming on a regular basis will be better if you do.

Competitive Sports

If your doctor advises it, you can gain relaxation through competitive sports. However, tennis, handball, baseball, football, soccer, basketball, and other such sports tend to make the average person more tense than relaxed. You can avoid a great deal of this tension by playing with other individuals who are also playing for relaxation. If you are playing against a fearfully competitive player, then his competitive spirit may infect you. This is certainly all right if you enjoy it, but if your goal is to relax, the competitive spirit will only interfere.

A good way to keep yourself relaxed while playing competitive sports is to use your affirmation. If you find yourself getting tense or angry during a game, silently repeat your affirmation while you are playing until your tension dissipates. If you are anxious either before or after a game, try using any of the Total Relaxation Core Techniques. You will find that five minutes of Total Relaxation will eliminate your anxieties.

Isometric Exercises

As a rule, it is a good idea to avoid isometric exercises, which include weight lifting and other forms of exercise in which you push and pull against any fixed object. They tend to raise the level of your blood pressure dangerously. If you already have high blood pressure, then isometric exercises can be fatal. Only perform them under the guidance of your physician.

Some Final Strategies

● The most important elements in exercising to relax are choosing the right type of exercise and learning to enjoy exercising. If you enjoy it, you will continue to exercise on a regular basis.

● Many people tend to overexercise when they first start. The first few days they have a lot of enthusiasm and exercise longer and harder than is necessary or safe. After their initial enthusiasm wanes, they give up exercising because they feel it is hard work. But if you exercise moderately to begin with, then you will enjoy it and continue on a regular basis.

● Some people find that it is more relaxing to exercise alone, while other individuals prefer to exercise with a partner or in a group. If you exercise regularly, you will gradually get to know the "regulars" at the gym, at the pool or on the courts. You may find that you enjoy working out every day with the same people.

● The purpose of exercise is both to relax and strengthen you. If you feel that you must constantly compete against others, relaxation will never dawn during your exercise and athletic sessions. The best athletes only compete against themselves. If you are constantly worried about whether you are going to win or lose, you won't play as well. Part of the energy you could have applied to winning is being dissipated in worry. Instead of worrying about winning or losing, concentrate on doing the best you can. You will gain much more joy from sports and exercise, and will perform better too. Your attitude, regardless of your physical capabilities, should be not to prove, but to improve.

● Don't be afraid of exercise. If you are uncertain as to whether you can exercise safely, consult your doctor. Then after finding a suitable form of exercise, start moderately and enjoy it.

TOTAL RELAXATION TECHNIQUE #6
SWIRLING LIGHT

Focus your attention upon the center of your forehead. Imagine that there is a slow but steady swirling of white light there. The white light is very soft and gentle. Visualize that this white light is slowly moving in a clockwise direction. Visualize that the swirling white light is slowly expanding. As it does, the white light begins to encompass the other portions of your body. Imagine the soft white light expanding in a circular swirling motion until your entire body has become lost in it.

Feel that the room that you are sitting in is becoming filled with the swirling white light. Visualize that the light is expanding beyond the room to encompass the building or area in which you are located. Then imagine that the white light is expanding even further to encompass all of the area for miles around you. Finally visualize the soft white light continuing to expand as it gently swirls around, until it has filled the earth, the sky, the universe, and all of infinity.

Let go. Allow yourself to merge with the slowly swirling white light. Feel that nothing else exists but this ever-present calm, peaceful white light. There is no yesterday, no tomorrow, no future or past. Your mind is calm and relaxed. All that exists is swirling white light, and you have become part of that light. Relax, continue to visualize the swirling white light, and experience peace.

Seven

Total Relaxation in Sleep

We are such stuff as dreams are made on,
And our little life is rounded with a sleep.
—WILLIAM SHAKESPEARE: *The Tempest*

It has been estimated that between ten and fifteen million Americans suffer from insomnia and other sleep related disorders. The vast majority of these sleeping problems are the result of stress. People try to overcome their sleep problems by resorting to prescription and nonprescription sleep-inducing drugs, hypnosis, biofeedback devices, and sleep clinics. Unfortunately, these artificial methods of inducing sleep cannot recreate the positive healing benefits of natural sleep.

The Quality and Quantity of a Good Night's Sleep

There is no real substitute for a good night's sleep. It is nature's remedy for tension and fatigue. After a good night's sleep you feel refreshed, alert, relaxed, and are happily looking forward to the challenges and opportunities of a new day.

Most people spend approximately one-third of their lives asleep. The majority of this time is spent in the dream state. Most people have many dreams each night, although upon waking they rarely remember any of them.

The ancients believed that during sleep the soul of the

dreamer left his body and traveled to other worlds. There it would consort with the souls of other dreamers, both from this and from other worlds. When it grew tired of its travels, the soul of the dreamer would return to earth and re-enter the body of the dreamer. Upon awakening, the dreamer would only remember fragments of his celestial journey.

Today we know little more than the ancients did about dreaming. However, psychological studies have demonstrated that dreaming is necessary for a person's mental balance. If people are constantly interrupted while they are dreaming, or not allowed to dream, they become hostile, withdrawn, and exhibit paranoid and manic-depressive tendencies.

For a short period each night while you are sleeping, you enter a dreamless state called deep sleep. When you are in this state, your brain produces more alpha and theta waves than it normally does while you are dreaming or when you are in a waking state of consciousness. While the significance of alpha and theta brainwaves is not yet fully understood, experiments have shown that human beings gain the most benefit from this part of their sleeping cycle.

Persons who suffer from tension and stress tend to spend less time in the deep sleep state than persons who are more relaxed. If you awaken from sleep feeling tired and exhausted, it is probably because you did not spend enough time in the deep sleep state. It is not a question of how long you sleep that will determine how much benefit you gain from sleep, but how much time you spend in the deep sleep state.

Most people tend to sleep much longer than they need to. The result is that they awaken from sleep feeling tired and groggy. On the other end of the spectrum are individuals who find it difficult to sleep for more than several hours a night. They are constantly nervous and tense because they can't get enough sleep.

If you don't find it hard to fall asleep or stay asleep, then chances are that you are sleeping too much. The reason that you sleep as long as you do is because you have been culturally conditioned to believe that you need to sleep a certain number of hours each night. The idea that you need eight hours of sleep each night is absurd. This is an arbitrary figure that may or may not apply to you.

The amount of sleep you need each night is influenced by the amount of physical and mental stimulation you are getting, the amount of stress you are subjected to, your age and the state of your health, your state of mind, and whether or not you are currently confronted with any special problems or difficulties that may be making special demands on your energy.

A good way to determine the approximate amount of sleep you need* is to deduct two hours of sleep from the amount you normally get. If you regularly sleep for eight hours a night, then you probably really need only six hours of sleep. If you sleep for nine hours, then you probably only need seven hours, and so on. Naturally this figure will vary from person to person, and will be influenced by other factors in your life that affect your sleeping needs; but the chances are good that if you sleep an hour or two less than you do now, you will feel better for it and have more of the one thing in this life that you can never get enough of, time.

Overcoming Sleeping Problems

It is important that you are satisfied with the physical condition of the room in which you sleep. Sleeping difficulties can often be accentuated by the color of your room, the type of bed or mattress that you sleep on, and also by the amount of noise and light that is present in your room when you are trying to sleep.

If you have trouble falling asleep, consider changing the color of your room. If your room is either too bright or too drab, it can agitate your mind. Most people find it easiest to fall asleep in rooms with light blue or light green walls. Try repainting your walls and see the difference.

Also, the darker the room, the easier it is to sleep. If too

---

*This figure will not apply to you if you suffer from insomnia or other sleeping disorders which prevent you from getting enough sleep.

much sunlight or artificial light enters your room when you are trying to sleep, purchase some dark window shades at your local department store. They should effectively eliminate any extraneous light from your bedroom.

It is essential that you sleep in a comfortable bed. A mattress that is either too hard or too soft can make it very difficult to fall asleep. Many people have also found that the height and position of their bed affects their ability to sleep. If you feel that your bed is not adequate, consider getting a new one. After all, you spend almost a third of your life in bed and it's worth doing everything you can to ensure that your time there is well and comfortably spent.

Another frequent cause of sleeping difficulties is noise. The sounds of televisions, phonographs, radios, people's voices, cars, trucks, sirens, trains, and other sounds can make it virtually impossible for you to get a good night's sleep. There are two alternatives to noise pollution: preventing the noise from penetrating the confines of your room, or blocking unpleasant noises with a pleasant alternate sound.

A great deal of the sound that enters your room can be blocked out by installing wall-to-wall carpeting, cloth wall hangings, soft furniture, and noise-absorbent ceiling tiles. All of these modifications absorb sound before it reaches your ears. If you have a bare floor, hardwood furniture, bare walls, and a hard plaster ceiling, then the noise that enters your room bounces off these hard surfaces and only becomes louder. Consider redecorating your room with sound-absorbent furniture and fixtures. You will find that it is much easier to sleep in a sound-free environment.

Another way to combat noise pollution is by masking the noise that enters your bedroom with a pleasant sound. Several devices are marketed that generate the sounds of the wind, ocean waves, and rain. Relaxation research has shown that these sounds make it easier for many people to fall asleep. The steady hum of a fan or air conditioner can also provide a soothing rhythmic sound that helps you fall asleep and effectively drowns out any outside noises.

Experiment with different types of sheets, blankets, and pillows. It is essential that you like where you sleep! Designer sheets are attractive, inexpensive, and can make going to bed more pleasant. Also try different types and weights of blankets. If you sleep with too many or too few blankets, the temperature will be unsuitable and it will be far more difficult to get a good night's sleep.

Your bedroom should be a restful and tranquil environment which you look forward to spending time in. A few modifications in the furniture, color, and arrangement of your room can make all the difference between a restless night of tossing and turning, and a good night's sleep. Consider spending a little time and money on creatively designing your bedroom. For example, one of the best sleeping investments you can make in times of dwindling energy is to purchase a goose-down comforter. Down comforters are light, warm, and save energy. Be creative with your sleep world.

Overcoming Insomnia

Insomnia is the chronic inability to sleep well. It can manifest itself in difficulty falling asleep, or in difficulty staying asleep. The vast majority of people who suffer from insomnia are victims of stress. By applying all of the strategies in this book, and by practicing the Total Relaxation Core Techniques on a regular basis, you will be able to eliminate your stress and get a good night's sleep. However, in some cases, people have had insomnia for so long that they have formed bad sleeping habits. The following strategies will help you to break any negative sleeping patterns that you may have developed as a result of your insomnia.

Strategies for Falling Asleep

● Practice any one of the Total Relaxation Core Techniques before going to sleep. If you still have difficulty in sleeping, then concentrate on Core Technique #7 Deep Relaxation, which is at the end of this chapter.

● Try reading for fifteen minutes before going to sleep. Reading something soothing will help to calm you before sleep. Try to avoid reading stimulating novels and magazines immediately before going to sleep. Instead, select a book or article about a pleasant subject which will not be difficult for you to put down.

● Before going to bed, talk to someone. If you are a chronic worrier or if you tend to have fears and anxieties running through your mind while you are trying to fall asleep, then get them out in conversation before sleeping. A few minutes of conversation either in person or on the phone with someone you care about can ease your mind and prevent you from worrying all night long.

● Resolve that you are going to get a good night's sleep no matter what. Refuse to allow yourself to worry or get excited about *any subject,* no matter how enticing it may be while you are trying to fall asleep. If your mind is agitated and you can't slow it down, then get out of bed and do something. You will only become more and more frustrated if you lie in bed tossing and turning.

● Try exercising before you go to bed. Take an evening stroll around the block or do some exercises at least a half hour prior to going to bed. If you exercise immediately before getting into bed, your exercising can stimulate your nervous system and make it more difficult to fall asleep.

● Try doing a half hour of yoga exercises before going to bed. Yoga is one of the finest forms of physical exercise and relaxation that there is. Yoga courses are inexpensive and are usually offered at your local "Y," community center, or health spa. It is not necessary to learn how to stand on your head or do any of the more advanced yoga exercises to benefit from it. The basic exercises, which can be practiced by almost anyone regardless of his physical condition, will make you more relaxed and help you to fall asleep. After completing your yoga session, always practice Core Technique #7 Deep Relaxation (page 137).

● Drink some hot milk or other soothing drink before retiring. But avoid drinking coffee, tea, or taking other stimulants for at least two hours before going to bed.

● Avoid eating too much before going to bed. If you eat late, it can be difficult for you to fall asleep, or your sleep will be unsettled.

● Don't go to bed hungry. Hunger will only stimulate your mind, making it more difficult to fall asleep. Try eating something light before going to bed.

● Repeat the following affirmation when you have difficulty falling asleep: "I am going to sleep well and wake up feeling refreshed and relaxed." Continue repeating this affirmation gently inside your mind until you fall asleep.

● Spend a few minutes in prayer or meditation before going to bed. Release your problems, worries, hopes, fears, and frustrations. Give them to God. Feel that God is taking care of you. No matter how difficult your life may be, or how many problems may face you, God will guide you through them all if you will allow him.

● Think of yourself as a small child with no problems, worries, or responsibilities. All day long you have played in the world and done your best. But now, regardless of how your day went, it is past. Feel that tomorrow will take care of itself. Worrying, planning, or scheming now will not change or improve the future. It will only make it difficult to fall asleep, and you will be tired and less capable of enjoying the opportunities that the next day will bring. Remember: "The past is dust. The future is now." Forget about everything except the moment. Feel that you are four years old and you are going to curl up in bed and drift off to a pleasant and enjoyable night's sleep.

Strategies for Staying Asleep

Many people are plagued with the problem of repeated awakening. If you wake up several times during the night, or if you awaken before you would like to and find it difficult to get back to sleep, then employ the following strategies:

● Use any of the preceding strategies for falling asleep if you awaken and find it difficult to get back to sleep.

● It is possible that you are awakening because there is something troubling you that you have not resolved within yourself. Mentally review any problems or difficulties you may be facing or avoiding. Once you determine what problem is bothering you, then feel that you will deal with it the next day. Practice one of the Total Relaxation Core Techniques and return to sleep.

● If you awaken from sleep earlier than you would like to, it is possible that you need less sleep than you think you do. One of the reasons you may be tired the next day is because you have psychologically conditioned yourself to believe that you need more sleep than you are getting. If you are unable to go back to sleep after awakening, even after employing the suggestions for falling asleep, then get out of bed and use your time constructively. Most of the great geniuses throughout history slept very little. From their point of view, sleep was a waste of time. They found that by sleeping only a few hours at a stretch, and by taking occasional naps or relaxation breaks during the day, they could happily exist on only a few hours of sleep a day.

Do not try to force yourself to get back to sleep. If you are awake and alert, then do something you enjoy. Many people find that the hours from midnight to sunrise are best for creative thinking and writing. Keep a good book or project nearby, and if you wake up, read or work. Allow your sleeping patterns to help you do and accomplish more. If you are tired after sleeping for only a few hours, then practice Total Relaxation Core Technique #7 Deep Relaxation. By practicing this technique for only twenty minutes, you can gain the benefit of several hours of sleep.

Fatigue Upon Waking
Very few people wake up bright-eyed and alert after sleeping for more than a few hours. It normally takes fifteen to twenty minutes to get the sleep and drowsiness out of your

consciousness. If you have trouble clearing your mind after waking from sleep, then try some of the following suggestions.

● Immediately upon awakening get out of bed. If you tend to linger in bed, then you will only remain drowsy.

● After getting out of bed do several minutes of gentle but active exercises. A morning run is also extremely effective. After your exercise period (or after getting up if you choose not to exercise), take a five-minute shower. Don't linger in the shower. The hot water may be soothing, but it will also make you drowsy.

● After awakening, if you have trouble in clearing your mind or in staying awake, try the following breathing technique:
Lie on your back. Place your right hand on your stomach and your left hand on your chest. Now completely exhale. Then breathe in, bringing the air down to your stomach. As you do this, the hand on your stomach should move upward as it is lifted by your expanding stomach. But don't breathe in at your chest yet. The hand on your chest should not be rising.
After you have taken in as much air in the area of the stomach (the lower lungs) as you can, then fill the rest of your lungs. When you do this, the hand on your chest should rise as your chest expands and fills with air. If the hand on your chest does not move, this means that you have already filled your chest cavity with air. Try to avoid doing this, concentrating first on filling the area near your stomach with air, and then filling your chest (the upper lungs) with air. Practice this a few times until you are comfortable with it.
Now try exhaling in the same way. After you have filled both your lower and upper lungs, then exhale first the air in the lower lungs (the hand on your stomach should go down), and then the air in your chest (the hand on your chest should

go down). Try not to exhale the air in your chest until you have emptied your lower lungs.

An easy way to remember this four-part technique is to memorize the phrase, "Inhale: Stomach-Chest ... Exhale: Stomach-Chest." If you practice this breathing exercise for five minutes, you will find that your mind will be clear and sharp and you will be fully awakened.

Oversleeping

The tendency to oversleep is usually a result of exhaustion due to extreme nervous tension. If you are constantly tense, worried, and anxious, then there is a continual drain upon your body's energy supply. One of the ways that your body may try to make up for this continual energy drain is by sleeping for longer periods. More than seven hours of sleep a night is probably more than you need.

If you are oversleeping because of nervous exhaustion, then try to minimize your exposure to stress. By applying the strategies and techniques that are contained in this book, you will gradually be able to reduce your stress level and eventually should not need to sleep as much.

Oversleeping can also be a form of escape. If you are faced with problems and situations in your life that place you under high levels of stress, you may seek to escape from them by sleeping. However, oversleeping will never solve these problems, nor will it eliminate the tensions and stresses that are depleting your body of its energy and health. It is only by learning to deal directly with the causes of your stresses that you will finally eliminate them. Otherwise, the same problems and difficulties that you are temporarily escaping when you sleep will still be waiting for you when you awaken.

It is easier to sleep less if you have something to look forward to. If you are bored or frustrated with your job, social relationships, marriage, or other situations in your life, then you may tend to sleep longer and avoid confronting the harsh realities of your life. Take a more active stance and strive to overcome the dull routines in your life that are causing you to oversleep. If you don't like your job, get another. If your social relationships are beginning to drag, make an effort to meet new and different types of people than you now associate with. If your marriage or any other aspect of your life is not what you feel it should be, take positive steps to change and improve it. Don't let your fears of change and the unknown cause you to stay with a life that doesn't satisfy you.

Each night before you go to bed, write down several things that you are looking forward to doing the next day. Even anticipating doing somewhat mundane things can help you to sleep less. Write down some new place you can go for lunch or the clothing that you are looking forward to wearing. List a project or job that you are looking forward to at school or at work, somewhere you intend to go after work, or something that you are looking forward to doing at home after work. Also consider things that you can do on the weekends that are educational or just fun. It is much easier to go through your work week when you have something to look forward to at the end of the week.

Don't complain about your lack of opportunities. Your life will be as interesting and exciting as you make it. Try exploring some new pastimes: roller skating, dancing, judo, calligraphy, new types of cooking, going out on a date with someone new, doing volunteer work at a local hospital or for some other worthwhile organization. By finding things that you can look forward to, you will become more enthusiastic about your life and you will be able to end your tendency to oversleep.

Strategies for Dealing with other Sleeping Problems

● Try not to use sleeping pills and other artificial preparations. Sleeping pills only treat the symptoms and not the causes of your sleeping problems. When you use sleeping pills, you are forced into an unnatural state of sleep in which you do not dream as much as you normally would. Your inability to dream can result in undesirable psychological stresses that will be exerted upon your personality by your subconscious mind.

Sleeping pills are both psychologically and physically addictive. They can also be extremely dangerous if used in conjunction with any alcoholic beverages. By using the techniques in this chapter, you should in time be able to overcome your need for any artificial preparations. Only continue to use sleeping pills under the recommendation and guidance of your physician.

● If you tend to have nightmares and other upsetting dreams that cause you to experience stress and emotional upset, then try creative dreaming. Before you go to bed at night, write down several dreams that you would like to have. For example, you might want to dream that you are enjoying yourself on a beach in Hawaii, or that you are going with friends to visit Egypt. You will find that with repeated practice, you will be able to direct the focus of your dreams. In this way, you will gradually be able to overcome your bad dreams.

● If you wake up from a bad dream feeling upset, then immediately practice your affirmation. Once you have calmed yourself, then try to realize that your dream had no reality behind it. Whenever you have a bad or negative dream, just ignore it. If you pay any special attention to it, you will only become more upset. Remember that it is only a dream, a product of your subconscious imagination. But if you have beautiful or inspirational dreams, then remember them. They can inspire you for days.

● If you repeatedly have the same dream or cycle of dreams, this may indicate that you are trying to work out a problem in your life. Resolve to face and deal with that problem. If you can confront and overcome whatever is bothering you, then your dream cycle will come to an end.

● Sleeping with another person can cause you a great deal of stress. If you are a sensitive sleeper, then the sound of someone else's breathing or the movement of his body can make it difficult for you to get a good night's sleep. Consider getting twin beds, or if necessary, sleeping in separate rooms. You might be surprised at the improvement this can bring to both your sleeping habits and your relationship.

● If you or someone you sleep with snores, then consider getting a humidifier. Often snoring occurs because the air in a room is too dry. A humidifier will take the dryness out of the air. It is especially effective if you have forced hot air heating.

● Ask someone who snores to sleep in a different position. People who sleep on their backs tend to snore more than people who sleep on their sides. With practice, they will get used to sleeping in a new position.

TOTAL RELAXATION TECHNIQUE #7
DEEP RELAXATION

This technique is an extremely effective method of relaxing the entire body. Many people find that practicing it for fifteen to twenty minutes will give them the benefits of rest and relaxation that they would have gained from three to four hours of sleep. If you suffer from insomnia or other sleep disorders, then practicing this technique can help you make up for a great deal of lost sleep. It is also especially helpful when you are in demanding situations in which you don't have the opportunity to get enough sleep.

Lie down on your back and assume a comfortable position. Keep your palms upward and your head in a straight, but natural position. Now, fold your hands into fists and tense every muscle in your body, just for a moment. Then, quickly relax. Relax all of the muscles in your body. Again, tense every muscle, making fists with your hands, curling your toes, and slightly arching the spine. Then, abruptly relax all the muscles. Take a deep breath, then slowly exhale. Inhale again, and visualize peace entering in through the top of your head. Exhale slowly, visualizing all pain, tiredness, tension, and fatigue leaving through the soles of your feet. Again inhale, visualizing peace entering in through the crown of your head. Again slowly exhale, visualizing fatigue, anxiety, worry, and tension leaving through the soles of your feet. Now relax and breathe normally.

Beginning at the top of your head, relax every muscle in your body, and every part of your body. Begin by relaxing the scalp, then the head. Relax your forehead, your cheeks, nose, mouth, facial muscles. Allow the jaw to sag, but keep the lips closed. Relax the back of your head, relax the neck and shoulders. Then relax your chest. Feel all of your ribs relaxing. Relax your spine. Feel your spine gently touching

137

the floor, and relax it vertebra by vertebra. Relax your stomach and lower back. Now relax your pelvis. Relax your abdomen, hips, and base of the spine. Relax your thighs, knees, calves, ankles. Relax your feet, toes, and the soles of your feet. Check over your entire body from the top of your head to the soles of your feet, looking for any signs of tension. When you find tense muscles, consciously relax them.

After you feel that you've relaxed all the muscles of your body, then turn your attention inward, to your internal organs. Your internal organs work very hard for you, both day and night, while you are awake and while you are asleep. They, too, need to relax in order to work more efficiently. Relax your lungs; allow your breathing to become easy. Relax the heart; focus your attention on your heartbeat to find that you can consciously slow down the beating of the heart, thus relaxing it. Relax your stomach muscles. Consciously relax the whole area of the stomach within the physical body. Relax the bladder and intestines.

Now relax your mind. Your mind should remain calm and alert, but totally relaxed. When thoughts pass in and out of your mind, simply ignore them. Imagine that you are a tiny bubble floating in an infinite ocean of peace and light. Now imagine that the little bubble of yourself, of your consciousness, is breaking and gently dissolving into the ocean of peace and light that stretches endlessly in every direction, never beginning and never ending. Feel that the little bubble of your consciousness now has totally dissolved and merged into the ocean of light and peace, and you have become the infinite ocean of light and peace, stretching endlessly in every direction.

Now, having completely relaxed the mind and body, simply let go and enjoy the peace of total relaxation.

Eight

Love, Sex, and Relaxation

~

Love does not consist in gazing at each other but in looking outward together in the same direction.
—ANTOINE DE SAINT EXUPERY

Whoever named it necking was a poor judge of anatomy.
—GROUCHO MARX

A young man once left his home in search of wisdom. He traveled far and wide and asked all those he met if they knew where wisdom could be found. Everyone told him that wisdom could be found at the universities. So he went to the greatest university in the land and sought wisdom there.

At the university, he asked the learned professors where wisdom could be found. They told him that wisdom could only be found in books. So he spent several years studying books in hopes of finding wisdom there.

But after reading and studying hundreds of books, the young man realized that he was no closer to finding wisdom than he had been when he first left home. Much to the dismay of his professors, he left the university and resumed his quest for wisdom.

The young man traveled far and wide and passed through many lands. One day, as he was entering a small town, he met a beautiful young woman on the road. She spoke with him and asked him where he was going. He told her that he was searching for wisdom. She inquired if he had had any luck. He told her that although he had talked with many

139

learned professors, read thousands of books, and traveled the earth, he had been unable to find wisdom. After listening to his story the young woman laughed at him.

"Why do you laugh at me?" he asked. "Do you think that it is funny that I have spent my life searching for wisdom?"

"No," she replied softly. "I don't think it's funny that you are looking for wisdom. For what is the worth of anything in this life without wisdom?"

After she finished speaking, she smiled at him and he noticed that there was a devilish glint in her eyes.

"Still you mock me!" he cried out. "If you know where wisdom is, then please tell me. Have pity on me."

"All right," she replied. "I will tell you. But if I do, you must agree to cultivate wisdom in the way that I suggest."

He nodded his head in consent and waited expectantly for her explanation.

"Wisdom," she began, "cannot be found in books. Nor can it be found by talking with learned professors. You may gain information this way, but you will never gain wisdom. Wisdom cannot be found by traveling. You may see the wonders of the earth, but you will not find wisdom. Wisdom can only be found inside your own heart. To give love unselfishly is the greatest wisdom that there is."

The young man had to agree that this beautiful woman had told him the true resting place of wisdom. He kept his part of the bargain and fulfilled her request. In accordance with her wishes, he resolved to look for wisdom only within his heart, and to cultivate wisdom by learning to love all those he met with a pure and selfless love.

Love: Conditional vs. Unconditional

Love can add new dimensions to your life. It can increase your happiness and give you the opportunity to share your happiness with others. Love can also make you miserable. It can cause you to become tense, irritable, anxious, depressed, and worried. The choice is up to you. If you choose to, you can love unconditionally and only receive joy and happiness from your love, or you can love conditionally and have nothing but heartaches.

These are the two principal types of love. When you love conditionally, you place limitations and restrictions upon your love. In conditional love, you always love someone *because*. You love her or him because of the way she looks, because of the way she makes you feel, or because of the things that she does to or for you. However, if the person you love no longer fulfills the conditions of your love, then you will withdraw your love from her. If she no longer loves you in the way you feel that she should love you, if she seeks to fulfill herself without considering you first, or if she chooses to ignore you, then you will become upset, angry, tense, worried, and unhappy. You will blame her for your unhappiness, feeling that if she had really loved you she would have treated you the way that *you* wanted her to.

When you love someone unconditionally, you do not put any restrictions or limitations upon your love. You love someone simply for the sake of loving him. Your love is not dependent upon someone else fulfilling you in the ways that you think that he should. You gain joy and happiness simply from the fact that you love him. Naturally, if he loves you and responds to you in a way that pleases you, you will be happy. But you will also be just as happy if he doesn't. Because you love him, you want him to be himself. If this means that he will love you in a way that doesn't quite suit your specifications, or if it means that he won't love you at all, you won't become upset. Your joy in loving is not dependent upon his reaction. You gain joy directly from your love and you require nothing else.

Whenever you love someone conditionally, you make yourself vulnerable to worry, stress, and tension. You do this by placing yourself in the Conditional Love Trap. When you love someone conditionally, you become dependent upon him for your happiness. If the person you love fulfills your preconceived conditions, then you will be happy. But if he chooses instead to be himself and love you in the way that *he* wants to, then you will be unhappy. The following chart will give you a brief overview of some of the more common qualifications and results of conditional love.

Conditional Love Chart

MAJOR PREMISE:	RESULTS OF UNFULFILLED CONDITIONAL LOVE:
I love you because you ...	If you do not fulfill the terms of my love, then ...
make me feel happy.	I will be unhappy.
turn me on.	I will be bored and unfulfilled sexually.
relax me.	I will be nervous, tense, and irritable.
take care of me.	I will be insecure.
support me.	I will be unloved.
are kind to me.	I will be unloved.
protect me.	I will be vulnerable.
make my life worth living.	my life will not be worth living.

Some Examples of Conditional Love

● *A mother.* A mother loves her son. She gives him everything that she can to help him grow up and become a happy and successful person. But one day he announces to her that he is leaving his job, marrying a woman she doesn't approve of, and moving to a distant part of the country. The mother is miserable. She tells her son that if he really loved her he wouldn't make her so unhappy. The son becomes confused. He is trying to be himself and follow his destiny, but his mother's conditional love makes him feel guilty. If he chooses to marry the girl he loves and move to a new state, his mother will be unhappy. If he chooses to listen to his mother and stay at home, he will also be unhappy. His mother's love has placed both of them under stress because of her conditions:

Loving me = Pleasing me in my own way.
Being yourself = Not loving me.

● *John and Alice.* John had been married to Alice for several months when he began to notice that she was saying and doing things he didn't approve of, such as getting a job because she was bored with sitting around the house. She also didn't like doing some of the things that John liked to do, such as going away on weekends to places that *he* had determined *they* would enjoy.

John was very selfish about sex. He felt that he should be the one to initiate all sexual activities. If he was in the mood to make love, they would, whether Alice wanted to or not. But if Alice wanted to make love and John did not feel like it, he would ignore her advances and go to sleep.

John decided that the best way to control Alice would be to punish her by withdrawing his love. When she didn't fulfill the conditions of his love, he would not speak to her for several days. Alice was not always aware of why John would act this way. Since John refused to discuss what was bothering him, Alice could only speculate as to what was wrong. By exhibiting this type of behavior, John placed both of them under tremendous stress. He was making a false equation with his conditional love:

> Loving me = Doing what I want.
> Doing what you want = Withdrawal of my love.

● *Susan and Tom.* Susan and Tom had been dating for several months. They both enjoyed being with each other and spent most of their free time together. Then one day, Tom announced that he wanted to be able to go out with other women. He told Susan that he loved her, but he felt that he was too young to settle down.

Susan became very distressed. Ever since she had been going out with Tom she had built her world around him. In her own mind, she had already planned the rest of their lives together. Tom's remark was a tremendous blow to her pride. Whenever she was with Tom, Susan would ask him questions about the other women he was seeing. She was constantly measuring herself against them.

Finally, Susan told Tom that he had to make a choice

between the other women in his life and her. Tom felt very bad because he loved Susan, but he didn't want to be forced into marrying her. He wanted to be sure he would be happy with her. He told Susan that he couldn't see her exclusively because he didn't feel he was ready. Susan responded by telling him that she didn't want to see him anymore.

Susan's conditional love resulted in unhappiness for both of them. Had she overcome her conditional love, she could have enjoyed Tom as a friend whom she loved and occasionally dated. But because of her conditional love, she stopped seeing Tom altogether. Susan's conditional love equation was:

$$\frac{\text{Loving me} = \text{Not loving anyone else}}{\text{Loving someone else} = \text{Not loving me.}}$$

Unconditional love can change your life and the nature of your relationships. It is not necessary to be unhappy in love. But as long as you feel that loving someone conditionally is necessary for your happiness, you will never be happy or satisfied with love.

The Conditional Love Cycle

People fall in and out of love. They meet someone, fall in love, and when that person disappoints them, they stop loving him or her. They feel that the person they loved has failed them. After time passes and they overcome their grief, they try to find someone else who will really love them. Again they meet someone, fall in love, and again they are disappointed. But instead of realizing that it was their love, not their lover that disappointed them, they will continue making the same mistakes and being unhappy in love. It is not love or the people they love that has disappointed them; rather, it is their wrong understanding of love. The following examples will make this clear.

Margaret had a number of boyfriends when she was in high school and, although she professed to love them, she was secretly dissatisfied with them. Throughout her youth, she had read romances in which happiness and true fulfillment always came to the heroine through romantic love.

But the boys in Margaret's high school were, to her dismay, typical boys. They were more interested in football than in chivalry. She decided that she would have to wait for college to meet her "knight in shining armor." But once in college Margaret was again disappointed. Although she was pretty and attracted a following, she still failed to find the sensitive, romantic, and courageous man she sought. She continued to go out with a variety of men, but she never found one man who could satisfy her.

After college, Margaret moved to New York. She went to work as an assistant editor on a magazine. At first, she tried dating some of the men in her office, but none of them measured up to her expectations. As a result, she became despondent. Margaret withdrew from everyone, including her friends at work. She felt that life was a cruel joke. She had decided that she could never be happy because no man could ever measure up to her expectations. Her continued stress and tension eventually resulted in a complete nervous collapse and several months of hospitalization.

Another example of how false expectations can ruin a happy relationship involves a young couple, Bill and Pat, who went out together in high school. They married after graduating and set up house in Chicago. Bill got a job working in a men's clothing store and Pat was hired as a receptionist for a Chicago television station.

But soon after the wedding, Bill started to grow dissatisfied with his wife. He felt that he had made an error when he had married her because she wasn't providing him with enough sexual satisfaction. Like many young men in our society, Bill had grown up with the idea that the most important part of a relationship between a man and a woman was "good sex." When his sexual experiences with his wife failed to measure up to his preconceived notions, he began to have affairs with other women.

But try as he might, Bill couldn't find satisfaction. He had affairs with many different women, but none of them seemed to satisfy him for any length of time. In the beginning he found that the novelty of making love with someone new was somewhat fulfilling. But after that novelty wore off, he was dissatisfied again.

Pat was unaware of Bill's affairs, but she sensed that there was something missing in her relationship with her husband. She resolved to try harder to make Bill happy, but try as she might, things only seemed to get worse.

Pat tried to talk to Bill about his unhappiness with their marriage. But Bill felt so guilty about his extramarital affairs that he couldn't discuss his dissatisfaction with his wife. Whenever she tried to speak with him, he would either tell her that he "didn't want to talk about it now," or he would deny that anything was bothering him.

As time went on, Bill began to abuse his wife. He criticized her, was unnecessarily rough with her, and took out all his frustrations on her. Finally the stress was too much for Pat to bear and in order to preserve her own happiness, she left her husband.

At first Bill was glad that his wife had left. But as time passed, he realized that he had lost the woman he loved the most. He finally came to realize that it was not that Pat had failed to satisfy him—after all, he found that no one else did either—but his own belief that it was up to someone else to make him sexually satisfied. He had placed too much emphasis on what he could get from someone else, rather than what he could give them. Unfortunately, he realized his error too late. But he resolved not to make the same mistake again.

The Art of Unconditional Loving

In order to love unconditionally and gain more satisfaction from your love, you must rid yourself of your wrong conceptions of love. The most popular of these misconceptions is that someone else will make you happy. Would that it were true! *Love can never make you happy.* Only you can make yourself happy. Love can add to your happiness, but as long as you think that love can make you happy, you will be a slave of love.

If you love someone and are dependent upon him or her for your happiness, then you are binding yourself to that person. This means that you are under his control. The threat of losing him will cause you to do everything in your power to keep him with you. In short, you have become a love addict. But ask yourself, is this what real love is all about?

The art of loving is the art of giving love. When you give a present, must you receive a present in return in order to be happy? No, of course not. Giving is happiness itself. You are happy because you have been able to give someone something. This is stress-free giving. When you expect something, you have ruined the act of giving. Instead of being an unconditional giver, you are being an entrepreneur who insists on getting a return on his investment.

Do you want others really to love you and stay with you? Then simply love them. When you try to bind others with your love, then they feel pressured and resist you. But when you love someone without conditions, she is drawn to you by the virtue of your love. The only real force that can compel love is love. If you love others unconditionally, then you will never be unloved. It is an old but true rule: "The more love you give, the more love you will receive." But the trick is, you don't give to receive. You give just because it gives you joy to give.

Unconditional love is not a mythical type of love that could only exist in an ideal society. Unconditional love is perfectly real and much more durable than conditional love. When you love someone conditionally, then when the going gets tough, you stop loving him. But when you love someone unconditionally, your love will brave any opposition. Shakespeare was well versed in both unconditional and conditional love. His most famous sonnet discusses unconditional love:

Let me not to the marriage of true minds
Admit impediments. Love is not love
Which alters when it alteration finds,
Or bends with the remover to remove:
Oh, no! it is an ever-fixed mark,

That looks on tempests and is never shaken;
It is a star to every wandering bark,
Whose worth's unknown, although his height be taken.
Love's not Time's fool, though rosy lips and cheeks
Within his bending sickle's compass come;
Love alters not with his brief hours and weeks,
But bears it out even to the edge of doom.
If this be error and upon me proved,
I never writ, nor no man ever loved.

It is not easy to love unconditionally, particularly when you have been brought up in a society which stresses conditional love. But slowly and surely you can learn to love unconditionally. When you do, you will receive much more joy from your love than you do now, and little or no stress.

Strategies for Overcoming Conditional Love

Try loving unconditionally. You can definitely do it. But don't expect that you are going to overcome the habits of a lifetime in a few short days. Don't fight against your conditional love. If you struggle against your conditional love, you will be like a man trapped in quicksand. The more you struggle, the deeper you will sink. Instead, practice the following strategies. Eventually your unconditional love will be strong enough to push aside your conditional love.

● Consider all of your relationships in terms of conditional and unconditional love. Make a list of the people you love and the conditions that you have stipulated for your love. Look at your list and realize how absurd your conditions are. Ask yourself if they really have anything to do with what you truly feel for the people you love. Forget your conditions and love simply for the sake of love.

● Stop looking at your relationships in "what's in it for me" terms. If your only concern is looking out for number one, all you will have is your own self-love. Be daring: try loving someone who cannot possibly give you anything that you need or want, except, perhaps, her love.

● Learn to overcome possessiveness and jealousy. When you are possessive and jealous you inhibit your ability to love. The best way to overcome jealousy is to realize that you are not dependent upon the person you love. As long as you feel that you *need* someone or that you *must* have him, you are bound to become jealous if there is any threat to your relationship. But when you love someone not because you need him, but because you love him, then jealousy loses its power.

● Try to "think love" less and "feel love" more. In our society we tend to over-intellectualize love instead of experiencing it. Don't worry if your love is irrational. If it's real love, then it is irrational! Don't become a slave to what is rational. Computers are totally rational, and totally devoid of love.

● Avoid falling in love with the idea of love. Don't feel that you have to be madly in love with someone all of the time, or that if you are not in love with someone, there is something wrong with you. Real love happens by itself. It's nothing that you can decide to experience. Don't force it. Let love come as it will, when it will.

● Be open to loving in new ways. When people you love do something that doesn't please you, instead of turning them off or getting angry with them, feel grateful to them. Be grateful that they are the way they are and you are the way you are. If they fulfilled all of your expectations, then they would not be themselves, they would be you. Love the people in your life for what they are, not for what they do. Allow them to be themselves and they will love you all the more for it.

● Try to see things from the point of view of the person you love. It is easy to get caught up in your own difficulties and to forget that the problems of others are just as immense as your own. Take time to step outside of yourself and see life from their point of view. It will make communicating much easier if you do.

● Don't let your love become old and boring. If your love is going to flower continually, then you have to renew it every day. One of the best ways to keep your love from becoming stagnant is to spend time with someone you love in new circumstances. New situations that you encounter together will add strength and freshness to your relationship. Try visiting new places together. Your sojourns need not be distant, time consuming, or expensive. But make sure that neither of you has ever been there before.

● Try to recapture the feelings you had when you first fell in love—it was probably unconditional love. You should still feel the same way. When you are with the person you love, reflect back upon the first time you felt you loved him. Try to remember as many specific images as you can: where you were, the time of day, if anyone else was present, the clothing you were both wearing, and so on. You will find that you can rekindle the unconditional love you originally had by practicing this simple exercise.

● Try to avoid hurrying through conversations with people you love. Learn to listen more and speak less. If you talk more than you listen, you will know a great deal about yourself, but very little about the person you love. Your time is the most precious commodity you have. Loving people means sharing your time with them. Take the time to listen to what they have to say. Even though you may immediately understand a point they are trying to make, instead of hurrying them through it, sit back and listen. Forget what they are saying for a moment and just look at them. Feel your love for them. Be grateful that you can love them and that they also love you. You are probably much luckier than you realize. Reflect on your good fortune and allow your emotions to climb into a higher and deeper love.

● Avoid the fear of "getting burned." If you have been hurt in love, then it is your own fault. If you had not placed any conditions upon your love, no one could have hurt you. If you had loved her the way she was, you would have been happy regardless of what she did. Instead of being afraid, try loving unconditionally. Don't expect to perfect unconditional love right away. Be content to make slow but steady progress.

● Speak openly with the people you love. If there is someone you love, then take the time to tell him so. Don't assume that he knows that you love him because you pay the bills or do things for him. Food, shelter, and clothing are nice, but they are no substitute for love. Take the time to tell people you love them. If you don't express your love, you are being a miser.

● Don't put off being with the people you love. If you put off seeing them or doing things with them because there are too many "important" or "pressing" things to do, you are making a mistake. Tomorrow there will probably be just as many things to take up your time as there are now. In some cases, tomorrow may not come. Death can claim those you love when you least expect it. Don't be like the man in one of my seminars who always meant to visit his father but never did. For many years he was very active and rarely visited his father, always assuming that eventually he would have enough time. His father died unexpectedly one night. At his father's funeral, he realized that he could have visited his father if he had made the time.

● If you don't have time to visit people you love, then call them on the phone or write them a letter. Give them a present for no other reason except that you love them. Delight in the people in your life. It's just as easy to love them as it is to find fault with them. Learn to love them unconditionally, a little at a time.

Sex: The Act of Love, Not Stress!

Unless you have chosen celibacy as a way of life, you are subject to both the satisfactions and frustrations of sexual love. Unfortunately, for most people the frustrations often outweigh the satisfaction. But the majority of stresses and tensions that are associated with the act of love can be avoided if both you and your partner take an active interest in making love, not stress.

The majority of stresses that occur to people when they make love stem from their misconceptions about what is expected from them. The most destructive of these tension-provoking attitudes is the macho need to "prove yourself." The idea that sexual performance is quantifiable and measurable is absurd. Yet people persist in alienating themselves from their partners because they believe that they must impress, overwhelm, exhaust, conquer, and multiple-orgasmatize the person they are making love to.

In fact, if you seek to make love *to* your partner, then you will both experience stress. If you seek to make love *with* your partner, then you can avoid stress. Making love to your partner means that you view making love as you would any conquest. Instead of allowing your love-play to take its own course, you are going to approach making love as a performance in which you are the star and your partner is the audience. If you perform well, then your show will be a hit and get rave reviews. If you perform badly, then your show will get poor reviews and close in Boston.

Another problem occurs when one partner reacts to the performance of the other. If, for example, one person feels that he must perform well and cause his partner to be thrilled and delighted with him, he places his partner in a stressful situation. If his partner fails to be impressed with his performance, he will feel as if he hasn't performed well. So his partner also has to perform and pretend that she was more thrilled than she really was. Thus both partners are performing and trying to be something they are not. The result of their dual performances will be stress. They will both be under stress to please each other through the strength of their performances, and neither of them will be relaxed or able to enjoy making love because they will be so busy performing, or trying to outperform each other.

The idea that the more potent a man or woman is in the bedroom, the more potent he or she will be in business, is absurd. To begin with, let's consider what being potent means. Is potency the ability to make love for hours on end? Or is potency the ability to satisfy someone sexually? Obviously it is the latter. But potency, in this sense, does not come from performing. The ability to fulfill someone is linked to loving, being sensitive, and being more concerned with making love *with* than *to* that person. The macho attitude of having to prove yourself will fulfill neither you nor your partner. When it comes to the bedroom, any performance is a bad performance.

The *raison d'être* behind tension in sex is that someone cares more about her or his own orgasm than she does about the feelings of the person she is with. As long as this is the attitude of one or both persons who are making love, then they will get very little satisfaction from their sexual encounters.

If you are interested in eliminating tension and frustration from your sexual experiences, then become more interested in giving than in receiving. Don't try to shape your sexual encounters simply to suit your own needs, with only a token regard for your partner's. Instead, be open and concerned with your partner's needs as well as with your own. This does not mean that you have to take a self-effacing or submissive attitude. It simply means that you love someone enough to allow your lovemaking to be an expression of your love.

Strategies for Eliminating Stress and Tension in Lovemaking

● Try making love without thinking about it. Just let yourself go. If you find that you are trying to "perform," then stop. Instead, tell your partner that you would like his or her help in learning to make love *with* him instead of *to* him.

● A great deal of stress and tension in lovemaking occurs when you hurry. If you are only interested in having an orgasm, you are missing most of the beauty of making love. Slow down and relax. Enjoy being with the person you love.

● Try not to expect anything from your partner. If you expect that your partner will make love to you in a specific way and he doesn't, then you will become frustrated and upset. Instead, allow him to express himself in his own way. Take a moment to tell him what you would like him to do. It's pointless to be embarrassed once you're in bed with someone.

● Love will heighten your physical lovemaking. If you have sex with someone simply for the sake of sex, then you will probably be disappointed with your experience. If you are making love out of habit, or simply because it is expected of you, or you expect it of yourself, then you will incur less stress by not making love. Only make love if both you and your partner really want to.

● After making love, don't stop feeling love. Often the most important communication between lovers occurs after the sound and the fury have passed. In the silence between you, you can fathom the depths of each other's being. If you keep on loving, then your experience will be much more fulfilling.

● Try being more concerned with your partner's experience than your own experience. Consciously separate yourself from your own desires and become sensitive to the person you are with. This may be difficult the first few times you try it, but eventually you will find that giving can be much more fulfilling than receiving.

● Avoid overemphasizing physical love. Lovemaking has its place in a marriage or other relationship. But it should not be the dominant force within a relationship. If you expect that every time you go to bed with your partner, the earth will move and complete fulfillment will be yours, then you are creating false expectations that are bound to be frustrated. Try opening yourself to enjoying whatever happens.

● Try to avoid routines in your lovemaking. Be creative and inspirational. If you always make love at the same time, in the same room, or in the same way, then your boredom with lovemaking can create unnecessary tension between you and your partner.

● Avoid feelings of guilt after making love. When you feel guilty, you are secretly indulging in what you have just done. You have nothing to be ashamed of. Feeling guilty will cause you to become tense and upset and destroy the beauty of your lovemaking. If you start to feel guilty, practice one of the Total Relaxation Core Techniques. After practicing the technique, examine your guilt. Consider if your guilt is going to make you a better person, or if it is going to make you or your partner happy. When you realize how pointless your guilt is, reject it. If you feel guilty again, repeat the same procedure. By continuing to do this, you will be able to eliminate your sexual guilt.

● Don't feel that you have to satisfy your partner through performance. If, after making love, your partner tells you that you didn't "perform" well enough, then tell him or her that it wasn't your intention to "perform." You are a sensitive and wonderful person. Educate your partner gently. Explain your goals in lovemaking. If you communicate your feelings about him well, your partner will probably respect them. But if he or she doesn't, then ask yourself if you really want to continue to make love with this person.

● Feel that each time you make love it is for the first time. Try to preserve your sense of awe and wonder at the mystery of life and love. Don't let your lovemaking become mechanical. Approach it with your heart and not with your intellect.

● If you do not want to become pregnant, use birth control. The amount of tension that an unwanted pregnancy can cause both you and your partner is unimaginable. Don't assume that you won't get pregnant because it is the wrong time of the month, or because the moon is in a particular phase. Worrying about whether or not you will become pregnant while you are making love can take all the joy out of your experience. Visit your doctor or local birth control clinic and get some advice on contraception. Then put that advice into practice.

● Many people incur a great deal of stress and tension because they make love when they really don't want to. Remember, it's your body and you have the right to do with it as you will. You are foolish to make love out of obligation, social pressure, or in an attempt to improve your relationship with someone. As a result of this behavior, you may start to resent your lover. You will not enjoy lovemaking and your experiences will severely damage your relationship. Only make love if your heart tells you to. Otherwise, you will lose your self-respect and place yourself under unnecessary stress.

TOTAL RELAXATION TECHNIQUE #8
THE WHITE BIRD

Picture yourself as a beautiful white bird. Feel that you are flying high up in a cloudless sky. Imagine that you are gently flapping your wings and flying higher and higher until the earth fades from your sight.

Now try gliding. Feel that you are floating on the air currents high above this world. Imagine yourself soaring and then swooping down. Feel the perfect freedom of unobstructed flight. You are flying alone high up in the sky. You have flown beyond all of your problems, worries, and difficulties.

Fly higher, beyond the sky into space. Fly between the stars and planets. Glide beyond all of the distant heavens until you have flown beyond time and space. Continue flying into worlds unknown.

Feel that you are flying now into other dimensions. You are passing through dimension after dimension. Each dimension is a different reality and you have glimpses of that reality as you pass through it. Feel that you are flying through hundreds of different dimensions each minute.

As you fly through each dimension, notice your bird body changing. It will assume a different shape in each dimension. Then, after flying through all of existence, return to this world. Fly high up in the sky and then swoop down to your home.

Fly back into your room and observe your body as it relaxes. Now re-enter your body. As you do, feel that you are bringing back with you a totally new perspective on existence. All of the freedom and vision you gained from your flight will stay with you now. You have experienced perfect freedom in flight. Your flying has totally relaxed and refreshed you.

Nine

Special Methods of Relaxing the Body

Happiness is not being pained in body
or troubled in mind.
—THOMAS JEFFERSON

Think of your body as one of your best friends. Would you make one of your best friends work for you all the time without rest? Would you place one of your best friends under continual pressure and stress without relief? Would you become angry with your friend when, after constant abuse, he began to break down? Of course not. Yet every day people abuse their bodies by placing them under continual stress without relief. Then, when they see their physical health failing, they blame their bodies which have tried hard to meet all of their needs and demands.

Your body has limitations. It can only endure stress for a specific amount of time before it will be injured. It can only work without relaxation for relatively short periods of time. You must learn to take care of your body in the same way that you would any piece of equipment on which your life and mobility depended. Your body's demands are not exorbitant. It requires food, shelter, sleep, exercise, and relaxation. But if you omit any of these requirements, your body will only be able to operate for a limited period of time before it is damaged.

You may be facing a personal energy crisis. You are tired, nervous, uncomfortable, unhappy, and more susceptible to disease because of a shortage of energy. But your problem is not the production of energy. Each day your body produces all of the energy you need. The reason you feel fatigued and are susceptible to stress is that you waste most of your life energy in needless worry and physical tension.

When your muscles are constantly tense and tight they are expending energy. When they are relaxed, they conserve energy. Try making a fist and holding it as tightly as you can for several minutes. Observe how tired you have become. Now relax your hand. After several minutes have passed you will begin to feel stronger. The same principle is at work within your body. When you are tense, all of your muscles are constantly expending energy. When your muscles are relaxed, they are conserving energy.

Make it a point to become more conscious of your body. During an average day, every hour or so check over your body for signs of tension. When you encounter tense muscles, consciously relax them. If you practice doing this for several weeks, the process will become automatic and you will significantly reduce your energy drain.

Headaches, stiff and tense body parts, eyestrain, and fatigue can be avoided if you overcome your tendency to tense your muscles. Your body does not have an unlimited supply of energy. Tensing your muscles for even short periods of time can make you feel tired and fatigued.

Progressive Relaxation

Progressive Relaxation is a Total Relaxation Technique which can be used to cut back on your body's energy drain. It is easy to apply, and can be used in most situations. Whenever you find yourself tensing your muscles, temporarily stop whatever you are doing. Then, just for a moment, make those muscles which are tense even more tense. Consciously make them as tense as you can. Next, take a deep breath, exhale, and slowly relax them. After doing this, if you find that your muscles are still tense, repeat the exercise. If you do this two or three times, you will relax your muscles and put an end to your energy drain.

The preceding technique works particularly well with muscles that have been tensed for only a short period of time. However, if you have gone through a whole day of tension without taking time to relax your body, it may be necessary for you to use more sophisticated methods of muscle relaxation.

There are four principal techniques that can be applied for relaxing muscles that have been tensed for prolonged periods of time: massage, applied heat, movement, and conscious muscle relaxation. Each method works well. Your application of them can vary to suit your own circumstances and needs.

The Art of Massage

Massage is an ancient healing art that is highly effective for relaxing tense muscles. Simple massage techniques can be applied by a novice with a minimum of instruction. However, advanced massage techniques, *including any type of spinal manipulation*, should only be performed by a licensed physical therapist, masseuse, or chiropractor.

A widely used type of massage is the whirlpool bath. When you sit in a whirlpool bath, the warm, swirling water causes your muscles to relax. At the same time, it stimulates your circulation, allowing more blood to reach any injured or aching parts of your body.

Simple massage should be more than sufficient for relaxing your tense muscles. You can do a limited amount of simple massage to your own legs, arms, neck, and facial muscles. But, for best results, it is desirable to have your body massaged by another person. As long as you are massaging any part of your own body, you will be using your muscles. But when you allow someone else to massage you, you will be able to relax your entire body.

While you are being massaged, it is a good idea to practice one of the Total Relaxation Core Techniques. This will ensure that you do not unconsciously tense your muscles during massage.

Frame of Mind

It is extremely important that whoever is giving you a massage should be in a quiet and relaxed state of mind. If your masseuse is tense and irritable, he or she will not be able to give you an effective massage. All he will do is transfer his tension into you. For this reason, it is a good idea to have whoever is giving you a massage practice a Total Relaxation Core Technique for several minutes before starting to massage.

During massage, it is important to keep your mind free from distractions. If you find yourself starting to think about *anything* other than relaxation, consciously reject the thoughts. It is best to practice one of the Core Techniques, or simply to let your mind drift. For the duration of the massage keep your mind centered on relaxation.

Position

For a full-body massage it is usually best to lie on a firm surface such as a bed or carpeted floor. If you are going to use a lubricant, then place a clean towel or sheet underneath you. Part way through the massage, you may wish to turn over to allow your masseuse to massage other parts of your body. However, the majority of muscles that will require massage can be reached while you are lying face down.

Technique

If you are giving the massage, then remain relaxed. If you are massaging someone with particularly dry skin, you may want to use skin cream or oil as a lubricant. Try not to be mechanical in your massage; allow yourself to be as spontaneous as possible. If you are in a calm and relaxed state of mind, you will automatically sense which part of the person's body requires the most attention, and you will automatically rub that person in the "right direction."

Massage is a highly individual art. Each time you give a massage, you should first ask the person you are massaging which muscles are tense, and if he or she has any sensitive spots or injuries that you should avoid. Then gently begin to rub those parts of the body which are the most tense. Gradually you can deal with other sets of muscles which may also be tense.

Strategies for Simple Massage

• Make sure that the temperature of the room you are in is warm enough. A cold room will only cause the person being massaged to tense his or her muscles, greatly reducing the benefit of the massage.

• If the person being massaged is exceptionally tense or nervous, try playing some quiet, soothing background music during the massage.

• Do not sit on the back of the person you are massaging! You may damage his spine, and the weight of your body upon his will cause him to tense many of his muscles.

• Do not pound, manipulate, twist, or in any other way be rough with the person you are massaging. Do not think of massage as it is portrayed in the movies. Hitting and pounding someone's back, neck, and leg muscles may injure him, and it definitely won't help him to relax.

• Be methodical. Work in a general direction from head to foot or from foot to head. Avoid hopping around between distant parts of the body; this does not promote relaxation.

• Pay particular attention to the neck muscles, the entire area of the back, the leg muscles, and of course, the feet. Use both hands to gently rub the parts of the body that require massage. Swirl your hands in circles when rubbing the back. When massaging the leg, arm, and neck muscles, you may want to curl your fingers partially and try to feel the individual muscles. Then rub firmly but gently along the line of the muscle in the general direction of the heart. This will help blood in the muscles return to the heart, and will improve the circulation.

• If the person you are massaging experiences any pain,

immediately stop massaging her. Only massage those areas of the body which are pain-free.

● After you have finished massaging someone, allow her to lie still for several minutes. Then assist her in standing or sitting up. Occasionally, people who are massaged become so relaxed that they require several minutes to reorient themselves. Never rush them or you will detract from the benefits of their massage.

● After receiving a massage, have a warm drink or some fruit juice. However, it is generally a good idea to avoid eating a full meal for at least half an hour after a massage.

Applied Heat

Heat is one of the best muscle relaxants there is. When you have tense and taut muscles, you can use heat to relax them gently and effectively. Heat can be applied to relax the entire body in a hot shower, bath, or sauna. If you wish to apply heat to specific muscles, then use either a heating pad or some of the "liquid heat" preparations sold in drugstores.

When you are tense, try taking a hot shower or bath. Do not make the water temperature too hot. If you do, you will find it harder to relax. Spending too much time in a hot shower, bath, or sauna will actually drain your energy. When you are exposed to heat, your body has to use its energy to cool off. As a general rule of thumb, ten or fifteen minutes in a warm bath or shower, or even shorter periods of time in a hot sauna or steam bath, will relax your muscles without draining too much of your body's energy.

Movement

There are a variety of physical movements which you can practice to help you relax tense muscles. Probably the best is yoga. Yoga exercises, when correctly learned, enable you to stretch your muscles to relax them.

Most exercises require a great deal of muscular power.

When your muscles work, lactic acid forms. Lactic acid build-up causes muscle pain, and you feel tired and fatigued. However, in yoga exercises, since there is so little physical exertion, there is a minimal build-up of lactic acid within the muscles. At the same time, yoga exercises relax you and allow you to store energy. For these reasons, many persons find that they have more energy after they finish doing a set of yoga exercises than before they started.

Noncompetitive swimming is also excellent for relaxing tense muscles. It is a complete form of exercise, utilizing many muscles that are not often used. The water supports your body and gives you an opportunity to use your muscles in a different way. Exercise in water, however, should only be practiced under supervision to avoid accidents and injuries.

Conscious Muscle Relaxation

The two most effective types of conscious muscle relaxation are deep, and associative relaxation. Both work equally well to relax the total body. It is merely a question of personal preference as to which you use, although many people initially find that deep relaxation is easier. Deep relaxation Core Technique # 7 is found on page 137. It is progressive relaxation of your muscles through direct and conscious attention to the muscles being relaxed. Associative relaxation involves the progressive relaxation of your muscles through color association. When practiced on a fairly regular basis, it allows you to relax your muscles in a shorter period of time, and can be practiced under more varied circumstances than deep relaxation.

Associative Relaxation
Associative relaxation should initially be practiced while lying on your back in as quiet and restive an atmosphere as possible. If the location you have chosen is noisy, try listening to music that you find relaxing.

Associative relaxation is a mild type of muscle conditioning. By associating different parts of your body with specific colors, and by learning to relax those portions of your body when you think of those specific colors, you will be able to relax different muscle groups just by thinking of the colors. For example, if you practice visualizing the color red when you relax the muscles in your legs, then eventually you will automatically relax your leg muscles whenever you think of the color red. By learning to associate different muscle groups with different colors, you will be able to isolate different groups of tense muscles and quickly relax them.

It is not necessary to relax specific muscles at the same time you think of a particular color. Simply think of a particular color for a few seconds *before* you relax a set of muscles. Then you can forget about the color and, instead, concentrate on relaxing these muscles. After practicing this once or twice a day for several weeks, you will find that you no longer have to think about relaxing your muscles. If you think of the colors that you have associated with your muscles, then your muscles will automatically relax.

While it is best to learn associative relaxation while lying down, after you have become adept at it, you can practice it while sitting, standing, or walking. If, for example, you have associated your neck muscles with the color gold, and if, while driving or engaged in some other stressful activity, your neck muscles become tense, then simply by thinking of the color gold for a few moments you will be able to relax your neck muscles and overcome your tension.

TOTAL RELAXATION TECHNIQUE #9
ASSOCIATIVE RELAXATION

Lie down on your back. Take a deep breath and slowly exhale. Relax. Think of the color green for a moment. Imagine that your feet, ankles, legs, knees, and thighs are being bathed in a beautiful green light. Now relax these parts of your body. Continue relaxing them until all tension has left.

Think of the color purple. Imagine that your stomach, abdomen, lower back, and lower ribs are being filled with purple light. Now consciously relax these areas of your body until they are completely relaxed.

Visualize your chest, upper torso, back, and ribs. Feel that they are being bathed in a beautiful light-blue light. Now relax these parts of your body until all stress and tension has left them.

Feel the area of your shoulders, neck, face, and head. Imagine that they are surrounded with a beautiful golden light. Now consciously relax these parts of your body until they are completely relaxed.

After you have completed this process, then imagine that your whole body is being bathed in a glowing white light. Now relax your entire body until all signs of tension have left you.

After you have practiced this technique a number of times, you will be able to use it to relax specific sections of your body at any time. For example, if you find that your stomach is tense while you are driving or at a meeting, then imagine that it is being filled with purple light. Your muscles should relax very quickly. If you develop a headache or a tight neck, imagine that this area of your body is being bathed in golden light. If you feel a tightness around your chest, then imagine that your chest is being bathed in a light-blue light, and so on. The more you practice, the better and more quickly the technique will work. Eventually you should be able to relax any part of your body within moments of visualizing the color you associated with it.

Ten

Special Methods of Relaxing the Mind

When you concentrate, you focus all of your energies upon the chosen phenomenon in order to unveil its mysteries. When you meditate, you rise into a higher state of consciousness.

—SRI CHINMOY: *Eternity's Breath*

The mind ought sometimes to be amused, that it may the better return to thought, and to itself.

—PHAEDRUS

Meditation

One of the best ways to relax your mind is through the practice of meditation. When you meditate, you completely clear your mind of all thoughts. As long as there is thought present in your mind, it can be difficult to relax. Meditation enables you to block out the destructive and negative thoughts that drain your energy and make you tense.

Scientific studies have shown that people who meditate have been able to reduce the level of their blood pressure significantly. However, to try and limit the scope and purposes of meditation to relaxation is to misunderstand its nature.

The Total Relaxation Core Techniques work somewhat differently than the process of meditation does. In meditation you seek to empty the mind of all thoughts and images. When the mind is cleared of thoughts and images a person is able to experience the underlying unity of existence—God,

Truth, and his own deeper nature. Relaxation is a by-product of meditation, not its goal. In Total Relaxation you use a specific group of archetypal image patterns to relax. When you use a Total Relaxation Core Technique it is not necessary to clear the mind of thoughts. You use specific types of thoughts to help you relax. The purpose of Total Relaxation is to enable you to overcome worry, stress, tension, and fatigue; it is not a vehicle for probing the deeper secrets of life.

Your mind is like a lake. If you want to see into the depths of the lake, then the surface of the lake must be absolutely calm and quiet. As long as the surface of the lake is filled with waves, it is difficult to see into its depths. In much the same sense, when you meditate you are seeking to make your mind absolutely calm and quiet so that you can see into the depths of your own being. As long as your mind is filled with thoughts, you will only see the surface. But when you have emptied your mind of all thoughts, images, and impressions, you will become fully conscious of your deeper self.

In meditation, there should be no thought or image in your mind, not even the thought of no thought. At first, this may seem difficult to achieve. However, with practice, you will discover that you can make your mind quiet and, for short periods of time, stop your thoughts completely.

Practicing meditation on a daily basis will give you great clarity of mind and will also help you to eliminate stress. Don't be discouraged if you have difficulty meditating in the beginning. If you didn't, you would be extremely unusual. In the beginning you are a beginner. Do not expect to become an expert overnight. To meditate well takes years of practice. Yet even within a few short weeks, if you practice on a daily basis, you can begin to feel the benefits of meditation.

Some Common Misconceptions about Meditation

Before considering the practice of meditation, let us review some of the more common incorrect assumptions about both the nature and practice of meditation.

1. *Meditation is dangerous.* Meditation is not dangerous. When practiced correctly, meditation will be of tremendous benefit to you.

2. *Meditation is expensive.* Meditation should always be taught for free. Anyone who teaches you how to meditate and charges you money for your instruction knows little, if anything, about real meditation.

3. *Meditation is linked to religious cults.* Nothing could be farther from the truth. Meditation is an ancient science which has been practiced by people from all walks of life for thousands of years. To try and restrict or limit meditation by saying it is associated with any one particular group of people is incorrect.

4. *Meditation is something that is easy to master.* Untrue. Meditation takes quite a bit of practice and dedication to master. However, if you are willing to put the time and energy into the practice of meditation, the benefits are great.

5. *You must have a secret word or mantra in order to meditate.* Nonsense. The highest type of meditation does not involve the use of a mantra at all. Mantras have their place in meditation, but they are neither secret nor essential.

6. *When you meditate, you are more susceptible to negative thoughts or evil forces.* On the contrary, when you meditate you are less susceptible to undesirable influences. If you are fully aware, it would be impossible for someone to sneak into your home. When you meditate, you are fully conscious, and it is impossible for any negative thought or evil influence to affect you. It is more likely that you would be subject to outside influences when you are not meditating.

7. *Meditation will cause you to withdraw from the world and become "spaced out."* No. As a rule, people who meditate take a more active part in everyday life than they did before they started to practice meditation. Meditation does not space a person out. On the contrary, meditation makes your mind quicker, clearer, and sharper than it has ever been before.

A Model for Introductory Meditation

1. Assume a comfortable position sitting up straight in a chair or on the floor. Place a candle on a small table several feet in front of you and light it. If you like, you can burn incense, or place some flowers upon the table next to the candle.

2. Start your meditation by chanting a mantra several times. A mantra is a specific word which, when repeated, enables you to silence your thoughts and to enter into higher states of consciousness. The most powerful of all mantras is AUM. Chant AUM out loud (pronounced OM), elongating both the "O" and the "M" sounds. Repeat AUM seven or more times before you start to meditate.

3. After chanting AUM, practice concentration for several minutes before entering into meditation. Practicing concentration will enable you to clear your mind, and will make it easier for you to meditate. It will also improve both your memory and the clarity of your mind.

To practice concentration, look at the flame of a candle. Look directly into the flame. Try to select a small portion of the flame to concentrate upon. Now keep your attention on the flame. When thoughts drift in and out of your mind, ignore them. If you forget that you should be concentrating, or you have any difficulty, don't become upset. No matter how many times your mind may wander, gently bring it back to the candle flame.

It is not necessary to think of the flame or to analyze its qualities. Only look at it. But look at it with intensity. Concentrate on the flame, but at the same time try to relax. Practice this exercise for three or four minutes.

4. Now you are ready to enter into meditation. There are hundreds of different meditation techniques, but no single best technique. However, the following one is extremely safe, effective, and easy to use. Practice it once or twice a day. You may not notice or feel anything different the first week or

two. But by the third or fourth week, you will begin to see a marked improvement in your ability to overcome worry, stress, tension, and fatigue.

According to meditative philosophy, there are seven meditation chakras (energy centers) in the body. When you focus your attention upon any of these chakras, it is relatively easy to stop your thoughts and enter into a state of meditation. The best chakra for beginners to meditate upon is the *heart center*, which is located in the center of the chest.

To find your heart center, try the following experiment. Hold your right or left hand out in front of yourself and extend your index finger. Now say the word "me" out loud and at the same time touch your chest with your index finger. Repeat two more times. You will notice that you will always touch your chest in approximately the same place. According to meditative philosophy, this is the location of your heart chakra (not to be confused with the physical heart which pumps blood).

Close your eyes and focus your attention upon your heart chakra. Keep your awareness centered upon this spot. When thoughts come in and out of your mind, ignore them. Instead, keep your attention centered upon your heart center.

After focusing upon your heart center for five or more minutes, you can stop. At this point, don't focus at all. Simply let go. Try to "float" on the sea of your consciousness. Don't direct your thoughts. If you find that you are thinking too much, then bring your attention back to your heart center until you have stopped thinking, or until your thoughts have somewhat decreased.

When you are meditating upon your heart chakra, you may notice several different sensations. If you feel very light, as if your body is floating, this is a sign that you are entering into meditation. You may also feel a warm, tingling sensation around your heart chakra, or you may be filled with feelings of peace, love, and joy. You may also see colored lights in different shades and hues. These are all indications that you are entering into a state of meditation.

Most people prefer to keep their eyes closed while they are

meditating. However, after you have been practicing for several months and are comfortable with your meditation, try meditating with your eyes half or slightly open. Continue meditating as you normally would.

5. After you have finished meditating, then chant AUM again several times. Chanting AUM at the end of your meditation session will help you to integrate your meditative experiences with the world around you.

6. After meditation, don't immediately enter into activity. Sit for a minute or two in silence and reflect on the experience you have just had. Often you will not feel the benefit of your meditation until several minutes after you have stopped meditating. If you enter into activity immediately, you can lose some of the benefits of your meditation.

7. Don't stop meditating. After you have finished meditating, watch your mind. When negative or destructive thoughts try to enter into your mind, stop them. Meditating each day will give you more conscious control over your mind. But it is important that you become more aware of your thoughts both when you meditate and when you are not meditating.

Your goal in meditation is to stop all of your thoughts. In deep meditation there should be no thoughts and no images in your mind. Your mind should be calm and quiet like a lake without any ripples.

In the beginning, it will be difficult, if not impossible, to stop your thoughts. The first few times you meditate, don't try to stop your thoughts, only ignore them. Instead, practice the meditation exercise that follows. After you have meditated for a week or so, then try to limit your thoughts. During meditation you can allow positive and hopeful thoughts to swim through your consciousness, but block out any negative or destructive thoughts. If you start to think of your problems, difficulties, fears, worries, or anxieties, push them out of your mind. Simply refuse to think about them.

After you have been meditating for several weeks or a

month, then try stopping all your thoughts. In the beginning, you will only do this for a minute or two. But gradually the time will build up. When you are able to stop your thoughts completely, you will be filled with feelings of peace, joy, and bliss. You may have many inner or spiritual revelations. Many people who meditate find themselves developing new talents, interests, and abilities.

Strategies for Practicing Meditation

● Always practice meditation when you are sitting up. Unlike the Total Relaxation Core Techniques, meditation cannot be practiced while you are lying down.

● When you meditate, you can sit in a chair, on a bed or couch, or on the floor. You can lean against the back of a chair or other surface. However, it is essential that your back be kept straight.

● Do not eat for at least two hours before you meditate. In deep meditation, you will have little or no physical awareness. Eating before you meditate will make you too conscious of your body. If you are very hungry, eat something light or drink some juice. But try to avoid eating a large meal before meditating.

● It is a good idea to wash your hands and face or take a shower before you meditate. This will both wake you up and also provide you with a feeling of physical purity, which is essential for the practice of meditation.

● Try to meditate in a quiet, clean place. When you meditate, you may want to burn incense. Good incense contains aromatic oils that soothe the central nervous system. Try to avoid brands of incense that are too strong or have a chemical smell.

● *It is essential to practice meditation at least once each day.* It is better to meditate each day for a short period of time than to meditate every other day for a longer period of time. Your ability to meditate well is dependent upon daily meditation. Sporadic meditation will produce few if any results.

● Most people find it easiest to meditate once in the morning and once in the evening. If you start your day with meditation, it will be easy for you to stay energized all day long. It is easier to meditate in the morning because your mind is not yet agitated. Once you have started your daily activities, your mind becomes active and it is much more difficult to stop your thoughts and enter into meditation. When you meditate in the evening, you will be able to release all of the tensions and worries you have accumulated during the day.

● It is better to meditate intensely for a short period of time than to sit in a listless state of meditation for hours on end. In the beginning, it is advisable to meditate for ten or twenty minutes at a time. After a while, you may want to meditate for longer periods of time, but in the beginning it is best not to overdo it.

● Don't be concerned with whether or not you are meditating well. The only bad meditation is when you don't meditate at all. If you practice meditation faithfully each day, you are bound to make progress.

● After you have practiced meditation for several months, you may wish to seek further instruction in the art of meditation. In that case, you should select a meditation teacher or guru who suits your own needs and sensibilities. But be careful in your selection! Unfortunately, there are many false gurus. They charge a great deal of money for their instruction and provide misinformation on the subject of meditation. *Real meditation teachers and gurus never charge a fee for their instruction.* There are a number of legitimate gurus and meditation groups in America and also a number of books that will be of help to you in learning more about meditation. For more information, see the bibliography at the end of this book.

Humor

Humor is an affirmation of dignity, a declaration of man's superiority to all that befalls him.

—ROMAIN GARY

One of the best methods for relaxing your mind is to indulge in humor. The ability to laugh at yourself and to laugh at the world is one of the signs of mental health. When you find that everything is oppressing you, and you have been overcome by tension and worry, try laughing. If you allow yourself to be overcome by the negative aspects of life, then you have made a serious mistake; you are taking your life and your problems too seriously.

The next time you feel sad, depressed, or tense, go to a mirror. Take a good look at that poor beleaguered being who is staring back at you. Now feel very, very sorry for him. The poor thing, it would seem that all the world has turned against him. Continue looking at yourself. Now try loosening up a little. Look at the state you have worked yourself into, and over what? You are upset, miserable, and worried about things which you can do nothing to change. Try smiling and laughing at yourself. It may seem ludicrous, but you must admit that there is something comic about that person who is staring back at you. Smile at yourself. Go ahead—it won't cost you anything. Now try laughing. If you can laugh at yourself and your *gigantic* problems instead of always taking yourself so seriously, then you will immediately be able to overcome even the most severe tensions.

Try to laugh more at yourself and at others. But always mix kindness and understanding with your laughter. People who laugh at the misfortunes of others are confusing real humor with sick humor. Real humor will raise your consciousness and help you to overcome stress. Sick humor only lowers your consciousness and makes you feel worse for participating in it.

Your greatest enemy is depression. You can easily overcome depression through humor. Don't be so hung up and serious that you can't laugh at yourself. Whenever you find yourself getting discouraged and depressed, realize that you are taking life too seriously. In life there are times for seriousness and times for unqualified merriment. Try laughing more and crying less. You will have less tension and be a happier and saner person if you do.

TOTAL RELAXATION TECHNIQUE #10
THE FIELD OF LIGHT

Visualize a field that is surrounded by large trees on all sides. The field is in full bloom. Hundreds of wildflowers dot the tall green grass that is gently blowing back and forth in the wind.

The field is filled with the melodious and soothing singing of birds. You can hear several different types of bird songs all around you. The sky above the field is a cloudless cerulean blue. The breeze is slight and the temperature is comfortable.

Picture yourself in the middle of the field. You are lying on your back gazing up at the sky. All around you is life. You are basking in the sunlight, looking into the cool blue sky.

As you stare into the sky, feel transported. The boundaries of your awareness extend themselves and you merge with the field. Feel that you are one with all the life of the field. You exist in each of the beautifully colored flowers that are swaying gently in the breeze. You are part of the tall green grass. You are the melodious songs of the birds. You are all of the life that exists in the field and you are able to feel and sense all of the life processes that are taking place there.

The sky is above you. It stretches on into the beyond. Your awareness expands and you become part of the sky. Then you find yourself back in the field.

The field is filled with light. Everything seems to glow and radiate. The sunlight reflects off each flower and blade of grass and sparkles in thousands of colors. Each one of these colors is a part of what you are. You merge with them and become them.

All of the colors stem from one white light. You go back to your own source and become that light. Nothing exists but that white light. All things come forth from it and eventually return to it. For as long as you choose to relax, feel that you are the white shining light that underlies all of existence. When you feel that you have relaxed for as long as you would like, imagine yourself coming back into the field. For a moment, pause and look around the field. Fix in your mind what everything looks like. This field of light is always waiting for you whenever you need to come to it. Remember it and come back to it whenever you need to. Then open your eyes and return, refreshed and relaxed from your sojourn in the field of light.

Eleven

Learning to Relax with Others

Your ability to relax with others is strongly linked to your ability to communicate. When you can effectively communicate with the people in your life, many of the misunderstandings, hurt feelings, and other factors that cause tension between you and those around you can be eliminated. In order to communicate effectively with someone, you must be able to relinquish temporarily your own perspective and be able to see things from his point of view. It is also important to understand that true communication does not usually take place with words, but in the silence between words.

Communication: The Art of Give and Take

Communication involves both expression and understanding. When you talk to someone, you are conveying ideas, feelings, and information. When you listen to someone, you are receiving ideas, feelings, and information. It seems, on the surface, to be a relatively simple process. However, if it were, then many of the arguments, disagreements, and other problems that occur between both individuals and nations would cease to exist.

In order to communicate with someone you must learn the art of listening. The first step in learning this process is to divorce yourself from any prejudices that you might have, either about what a person is saying to you, or about the person himself.

If, for example, a friend is trying to tell you about an ex-

perience he had, you must take a fresh and active interest in
what he is saying. You will do him a great disservice if you
assume that what he is telling you is not important. Listen
carefully to what he has to say, but at the same time do not
allow yourself to become so caught up in his conversation
that you miss other important things that he is saying without words. Not only should you listen to the meaning of his
words, but listen to his tone of voice. Observe his body lan-
guage. Is he tense and upset? Is he trying to tell you something that he himself might not be fully conscious of? Take
the time to look beyond the surface of his words and fathom
what he is really trying to communicate to you.

True communication takes place when you and the person
you are communicating with are able to drop your guards
and experience each other in a deeper way. In order to have
true communication, you must be as interested in someone
else's ideas as in your own. You don't have to be in agreement with the other person; you just need to be willing to
find out his or her point of view. When you learn to communicate effectively with others on both verbal and nonver-
bal levels, you will have eliminated much of the stress and
tension that takes place in your associations with others.

Communicating Effectively

In order to express yourself effectively, you must have a
clear understanding of what you are trying to say. If you are
unclear about your own ideas, feelings, and emotions, it is
going to be extremely difficult for anyone else to understand
what you mean.

One of the best ways to gain a clearer understanding of
your own feelings and ideas is to write them down. When
you see them on paper it will immediately become apparent
if they are sensible and rational. If all your feelings and ideas
are internalized, it can be difficult for you to gain the
perspective necessary to evaluate them.

Not every idea, thought, and emotion that you have is
worthy of communication. You probably know someone who
has the habit of saying everything that passes through his

mind. His constant chatter only creates irritation among those who listen to him. Few people have the ability to be entertaining and informative in their conversation all of the time.

Try listening to yourself more. You may be surprised by what you hear. If you hear yourself saying something to someone else that is inaccurate or incomplete, don't be afraid to correct yourself. Great people are always happy to correct themselves. They realize that the opinions others have of them are largely dependent upon what they say. If you are constantly misrepresenting yourself by not expressing yourself clearly, you will not only fail to communicate with others, but you will also paint an incorrect picture of what you are like. Don't be afraid to correct yourself when the occasion arises. Your modifications will bring about greater clarity in your communication. At the same time, it will show others that you are a comprehensive human being who is not so serious that you can't correct yourself.

Some Strategies for Achieving True Communication

● Take the time to listen to others. Monitor yourself in your conversations. If you spend more time talking than you do listening, you are not communicating well.

● Try to be relaxed when you are communicating with others. If you find yourself becoming tense and nervous, ask yourself why. Have they done something or said something to upset you? Are they in any way a threat to you? Practice your *Affirmation* or your *Ideal* (see Chapters 3 & 4) when you notice yourself becoming tense with others. If you cannot be relaxed with those around you, then they will find it difficult to relax with you. Without at least one of the communicating parties being relaxed, it is unlikely that true communication will take place.

● Identify with the person who is speaking. Try to see

things from his perspective and with his value system. If you can do this, you will find yourself automatically speaking to him in terms that he can understand. If you don't adjust your conversation to the range and level of your audience, you will fail to get through to it.

● Don't be afraid to open yourself up to others, or to allow them to reveal themselves to you. As long as you allow your irrational fears to keep you from experiencing someone else, you will have great difficulties in communicating with him.

● Don't depend on the other person to open up first. You start. If you show your own openness, people will quickly respond and open up to you. But if you wait for them to take the initiative, they may never do so. What you are trying to do is communicate. If you wait for someone else to take the initiative, you are only preventing yourself from accomplishing what you are setting out to do.

● When it is permissible, and if you are so inclined, touch someone. Pat him on the back, shake hands with her give him a kiss on the cheek. Often touching someone can create a bond of immediate communication and break through barriers which would not have fallen otherwise. However, don't overdo it. Try and be sensitive to the needs and sensibilities of the people you are with. Touching some people will only cause them to become more tense. Use your own good judgment to decide when physical contact will help you communicate.

● Learn to trust your feelings. If you get the feeling that someone you are speaking with is trying to communicate but is unable to, then help him. If you find yourself rambling on without saying what you really mean, then pause for a moment, and tell the person you are speaking with that you are not clearly expressing your feelings. Then try again until you have succeeded.

● Learn to be sparing in your words. Avoid talking simply

for the sake of talking. True friends can sit in silence with each other without becoming uncomfortable.

The inability to communicate causes a great deal of stress and tension. You must be able to express your feelings clearly. But how can you know what you feel? In order to find out, you must be relaxed. As long as you are under stress it is difficult to gain the proper perspective on your own thoughts and emotions. When you are unsure about how you feel about a subject, person, or choice you have to make, try the following exercise.

Write down on a piece of paper whatever it is you are trying to understand. If you find that you have difficulty expressing yourself when you are trying to write your feelings down, it is not because you are a poor writer, but because you are unclear about what your true feelings are. But regardless of how your thoughts may appear to you on paper, write them down anyway.

After you have finished, consider what you have written. Ask yourself if you have left out any important feelings or ideas. Also consider whether you are being honest with yourself. Don't write down feelings and emotions simply because they sound good. It's pointless to try to fool yourself. Be honest! Write down what your true feelings are.

After you have ascertained that these are your true feelings, then practice one of the Total Relaxation Core Techniques or the meditation technique. While you are practicing a core technique, do not allow yourself to think about the subject that you are trying to clarify. A few more minutes of thought is not going to give you any new insights on the subject.

After you have finished relaxing or meditating, again write down your feelings about the subject you are trying to clarify. However, this time make sure that you write spontaneously. Don't pause to try to think about or evaluate your feelings. Simply write them down as quickly as you can.

Now compare the feelings and thoughts you have just written with the feelings and thoughts you had previously recorded. The difference between the two is the difference between what you *thought* you felt and what you *really* felt.

The thoughts, ideas, and feelings which you wrote down after practicing a relaxation or meditation technique will be your true feelings about a subject. If these ideas and feelings are similar to those you had previously written, then your original thoughts on the subject were correct. However, if there is a substantial difference in the thoughts and feelings you have recorded in your second writing, then opt for the second version.

Example #1: My True Feelings

Question: What are my true feelings about my husband?
Response: I love my husband. He doesn't always treat me the way I would like him to. Often he is unkind. But he is very good with the children, and he works hard every day to provide for us. I get mad at him, but when we are alone and things are going right, I really love him and want to be with him.

My True Feelings
(After Relaxation or Meditation)

Question: What are my true feelings about my husband?
Response: Before I married him I really loved him and I thought he loved me. But he no longer does. He stays with me because it is convenient. He really doesn't love me any more. We are staying with each other out of habit. It would be better if we separated or divorced.

Example #2: My True Feelings

Question: What are my true feelings about my job?
Response: I like my job. I was trained for this position and I am satisfied with it. I don't always enjoy the people I work with. Some of their ideas and conversations seem petty. I no longer feel excited about my work, but I suppose that's how it is with any job after a while.

My True Feelings
(After Relaxation or Meditation)

Question: What are my true feelings about my job?
Response: I love my work. The only reason that I have had difficulty with it lately is because I haven't been doing the job I should. I have been complaining just to avoid taking responsibility for my own shortcomings. The people I work with are very nice. If I would try harder, I could get along with them. But it is easier for me to find fault with others than to do something about improving my relationships with them.

Problem Solving

The same method can be employed for decision making and problem solving. Don't agonize over decisions you have to make or problems you must solve. If you do, you will only create unnecessary stress and tension for yourself. Instead, write down the problem you are trying to solve or the decision you are attempting to make and employ the same technique described above.

While it is not absolutely necessary, it is a good idea to write down some considerations of the problem you are trying to solve. But do not evaluate these considerations when you make your final decision. Instead, rely on your immediate feeling after you have finished relaxing or meditating.

Problem Solving: Example #1

Question: Should I buy a new car?
Considerations: The car I have now is getting older. I will probably get more money for it if I trade it in now. I'm really not sure if I can afford the payments on a new car though. Suppose I lose my job? But my car takes too much gas. The price of gas is skyrocketing. It would be less expensive to have a small car that got better mileage.

Answer (after relaxation or meditation): *Yes.*

Problem Solving: Example #2

Question: Should I marry Susan?
Considerations: I love Susan. We have been going out together for over a year now. We both have good jobs, so we
can afford to get married. But I keep feeling that I am going
to be tied down and I'm not sure if I want to be. Maybe it
would be better to wait until I'm sure.

Answer (after relaxation or meditation): *Marry her now.*

Validity Test
How can you be sure that you have discovered your true
feelings about a subject, or if you got the correct answer to a
problem? When you employ the preceding methods, you are
allowing your inner self to make the decision for you. Often
the criteria we use to make decisions are totally irrelevant.
We clutter up our minds with them in an attempt to evaluate
our situation rationally. Let's say, for example, you are trying to decide whether or not to move to California. You write
down on a piece of paper all of the reasons for and against
such a move. If you have listed more reasons to stay where
you are than to move to California, your mind will tell you
not to move. But suppose there are both good reasons to go
and good reasons to stay? Or suppose that you just can't
make up your mind? If you continue to worry about what
you should do, you will only cloud your mind with tension
and lose your ability to make a good decision. The fact that
you have not been able to come to an equitable decision
indicates that you are not in touch with your true feelings.
But by practicing Total Relaxation or meditation, you will
be able to clear your mind and allow your true feelings to
come forward. You may discover that your true feelings have
nothing to do with the reasons you listed for moving or staying. Your true feelings may tell you to move to California
even though there are more "reasons" to stay home. If you
can follow your true feelings you will be happy, relaxed, and
successful. Most good decisions and important discoveries

are not the result of a careful analytical process. They come in a flash of intuition from the depths of your being.

There is a simple test which you can use to evaluate whether the answer you have gotten from your inner self is correct or not. When a correct answer or insight comes to you after practicing Total Relaxation or meditation, no other thought will be able to contradict it for several minutes. The answer will come with such strength and certainty that there will be no doubt in your mind for at least several minutes.

Also, once you have received the correct answer, you will have a feeling of relief. This feeling of relief is the sign that you have had true communication with your deepest feelings. If you do not feel relief when you get your inner answer, or if immediately following there are other conflicting thoughts that give you other answers, then you have not got the correct answer. If this happens, then try the process again later in the day, or the next day. Your mind was too agitated to allow you to know what you really felt. But if you try again later when your mind is more relaxed, you will be able to gain a correct sense of what your true feelings are.

Self-confidence

Relaxing with others requires self-confidence. When you are self-confident you can never feel threatened by anyone, regardless of how powerful or influential he or she may be. When you are self-confident, you feel that other people can only add, and never detract, from what you are. You are secure and happy whether you are with your friends and family or in a foreign land surrounded by complete strangers. Your self-confidence is not necessarily based upon extensive education or worldliness, but upon a correct assessment of your own innate human potential.

Insecure people can never relax with others. At every moment they feel threatened by the people they are with. Insecure people will usually try to overcome the stress of their insecurities and self-doubts, either through excessive approval seeking, or by placing an emotional block between themselves and the people in their lives.

Insecure people constantly seek the approval of others. This places an immediate strain upon their relationships. In the beginning of a relationship, most people don't mind giving someone else strength and support. But when they realize that someone is going to be relying upon them constantly, they often try to minimize their association with that person.

When you are self-confident, people are drawn to you. Because you are at ease with yourself others find it easier to be themselves. Occasionally, your self-confidence will be thought of as egotism by those who don't know you well. But if you intermingle gentleness with self-confidence, then anyone will find it easy to relax with you.

Insecure people feel that other people are a threat to them. They believe that it is necessary to get on everyone's "good side." They compromise their own beliefs in order to have the approval and friendship of others. They change their opinions according to the company they keep. If they are with a group of liberals, they adopt liberal opinions and espouse the causes of the common man. If they are with a group of conservatives, they support the conservative platform. But they never present their own opinions on a subject for fear that others will criticize or reject them.

A self-confident person likes all types of people. He can afford to, since he does not feel threatened by them. Insecure people tend to limit the depth of relationships for fear that others will take advantage of them. As a result, they tend to have few, if any, real friendships.

Self-confident people do not court the opinions of others. They don't really care if other people agree with them. They have a good sense of who they are and, whether it is good or bad, they would rather be themselves than try to be someone they are not.

Insecure people have lost touch with themselves. They have adopted so many different attitudes and personalities to please others that they have forgotten who they are. Most people find it difficult to relax around insecure people because of their constant nervousness. They also find it difficult to be around an individual who does not have enough integrity to defend his own principles and opinions.

If you want to improve radically your relationships with others, then overcome your insecurities. Practice the strategies in Chapter Three for overcoming fears, doubts, and insecurities. As you become more confident you will find it increasingly easy to relax with others. The more relaxed you can be with those around you, the easier it will be for them to relax with you.

Overlooking Shortcomings

Relating to and relaxing with others is an art. If you can learn to effectively communicate with others and be confident in yourself, you will have taken two important steps in learning this art. However, in conjunction with these two steps, it is equally important that you learn to be compassionate in your dealings with others. If you cannot find it in your heart to allow the shortcomings and lapses of others to pass by, you will not reach your goal of learning to relax with others.

When most people see imperfections in others, they either criticize them or offer them charity. In either case they do nothing constructive to help a person overcome his or her imperfections. They only manage to alienate themselves from the person they are seeking to help.

When you criticize people, you only help to reinforce whatever may be wrong with them, and thus make it all the more difficult for them to overcome whatever their problem may be. When you offer someone your charity, you immediately gain a false sense of superiority. For example, you may say to yourself, "John has an imperfection. Let me help him overcome his problem." But in effect you are saying "He is inferior because of his imperfection. I am superior because I can help him overcome his problem."

When you approach someone with charity, you immediately set up an imbalance in your relationship with him. You are playing the role of the good samaritan and forcing him to play the role of the inferior person who requires assistance. This attitude emotionally castrates the person who has the problem or difficulty, and causes him to resent the "good samaritan" who is helping him.

On the other hand, when you feel compassionate towards others, you do not feel in the least bit superior to them. You feel, instead, that they are extensions of your own being. You feel fortunate that life has given you the opportunity to help them. Your help is only given with sincerity and humility, and never with a sense of superiority.

If you want to improve your relationships with others, then view them with compassion and not with charity. If you perceive their shortcomings, then instead of secretly feeling superior to them, try to help them. The best way to help is to forget about their imperfections. By observing their imperfections, you only make it more difficult for them to change. The major obstacles that prevent people from overcoming their limitations are the preconceived opinions of others. When you tell people what is wrong with them, they may feel that their problems are insurmountable.

Some Strategies for Learning to Relax with Others

● The next time you observe the faults or imperfections of other persons, ask yourself if your observations are either going to help them overcome their problems, or help you relate better to them. The chances are they will do neither. Instead of spending your time observing the faults and imperfections of others, try to focus your attention on their good points and strengths.

● It is always easier to destroy something than it is to build. In the same sense, it is always easier to criticize someone and find fault with her than it is to compliment her. If you want to help someone relax with you, give her a compliment. Sincere compliments and mutual appreciation are necessary for any positive relationship.

● Instead of paying attention to the faults and imperfections of others, give a little more thought to overcoming your own inadequacies. The time you spend observing and criticizing others is not going to improve you or them. If you use the same time and energy overcoming your own shortcomings, you will have accomplished something much more worthwhile.

● Accept that people are imperfect, and love them for it. If your heart is big enough, you will make allowances for the shortcomings of others.

● If someone is unkind to you or says malicious things about you, instead of being upset or disappointed, forgive him. Relaxing with others means accepting both the good and bad in others. If a four-year-old child does something wrong, we don't feel that he will always do the same wrong thing. In the same sense, people can and do change. *Age is no barrier to change.* You can help people change by adopting a compassionate attitude towards their imperfections. But don't expect others to change according to your own preconceived notions of when or how they should change. Allow them to grow and develop in their own ways. If you allow people to be themselves without criticizing them, you will find it very easy to relax with others, and they will find it similarly easy to relax with you.

TOTAL RELAXATION TECHNIQUE #11
THE CLOUDS

Visualize that you are sitting on top of a very high mountain. The sky above you is filled with puffy white clouds. The banks of white clouds are gently drifting over your head. As you watch them you find yourself feeling very relaxed.

Feel that your body is becoming very light. You are so light that you are starting to float. Your body is rising above the mountain top and is floating up into the clouds. You are surrounded by beautiful white puffy clouds on all sides.

Feel that you are floating with the clouds. As you drift with the clouds you are losing track of time. Today, yesterday, and tomorrow have all merged together. All that exists for you is timeless floating high above the earth.

As you float in the sky you are conscious that you are passing over oceans, deserts, forests, and cities. You are above and beyond them all as you are blown forward by the winds of existence. Continue visualizing yourself floating with the clouds for as long as you like. Simply drift with the white clouds and relax ...

When you are totally relaxed, picture that you are again among the mountains. Visualize the mountain you were originally sitting on. Feel that your body is growing heavier and that you are drifting back down to the mountain top. Imagine yourself sitting on top of the mountain, completely refreshed and relaxed after your journey with the clouds.

Twelve

Life without Stress

Brooding and despondency are the worst foes to kill life in all its divine inspiration. No more brooding, no more despondency. Your life shall become the beauty of a rose, the song of the dawn, the dance of the twilight.
—SRI CHINMOY: *Eternity's Breath*

The longer I live the more beautiful life becomes.
—FRANK LLOYD WRIGHT

He who asks of life nothing but the improvement of his own nature ... is less liable than anyone else to miss and waste life.
—HENRI FRÉDÉRIC AMIEL

The totally relaxed person is able to accept all the incongruities of life and enjoy them. He has learned that it is both possible and practical to live a happy and fulfilled life in the midst of situations and circumstances that cause others to become upset, nervous, depressed, and immobilized. The totally relaxed person takes the time to enjoy his life. He has learned that the secret of life is not to struggle, but to smile.

The totally relaxed person takes life as it comes. He is not overly concerned with what happened to him yesterday, nor is he worried about what will occur tomorrow. He is actively enjoying today with all of its opportunities and challenges.

The totally relaxed person is more interested in improving than in proving. She is easygoing and free-spirited. At the same time, she recognizes the need for discipline. But her discipline is self-imposed. It is the discipline that is used to create and give form to life.

A totally relaxed person strives to overcome his limitations and perfect his nature gradually. He realizes that lasting changes and improvements do not occur overnight, but come about gradually through sincere effort. He strives to be a better person, but, if he does not change or transform in the way that was originally anticipated, instead of becoming upset he enjoys what he has become. He realizes that the guiding hand of life is constantly at work in his life. He is willing to help that hand, but also willing to sit back and let life take its course.

One of the signs of totally relaxed persons is that they are able to love those around them unconditionally. Instead of binding the persons they love with gifts and other inducements, they allow the strength and purity of their love to draw others to them. They feel that love is a gift that should not be given lightly. At the same time, they are free with their love. They do not give their love conditionally as a reward for services rendered. They give their love without seeking a return on their emotional investment.

They are unaffected by the environmental stresses that may surround them. Their own state of calm and tranquility has the power to negate the pressures and problems that are thrust upon them by the world. They view each problem as an opportunity to grow and become. They realize that all growth involves effort and that the effort itself is joyous.

Totally relaxed persons have learned to achieve a balance between work and rest. When they work, they keep their mind clearly focused upon the job at hand. When they play or rest, they actively participate in activities that stimulate but do not deaden them.

They have pushed aside their fears of change and the unknown. They are willing to experiment with their lives. They look forward to opportunities to meet new people or to visit new places. If they see that the place they live in, or the job they have is no longer satisfactory, they change it. They do not allow themselves to become prisoners of habit. They observe themselves and when they find that they are getting in a rut, they get out of it.

Totally relaxed persons take responsibility for their actions. At the same time, they do not take themselves too seriously. They are secure enough to be able to poke fun at themselves and to allow others to laugh with them. They realize that a smile can often erase even the greatest of problems.

They are committed to happiness. They know that the shortcut to happiness is helping others. But they are not overbearing in their service to others, nor do they threaten the dignity of the person they are aiding.

They delight in their own lives. They accept themselves as rapidly evolving beings who always have something more to see, something more to learn, and something more to become. When they make mistakes, they are not discouraged. They have learned that the only real success is continual progress, and are committed to their own self-development. They make time each day to work consciously towards their own self-perfection.

Summary of the Principles of the Total Relaxation Program

● The single greatest killer in the modern world is stress. People who underestimate the damaging effects of stress, and who do not take the time to overcome stress through relaxation, are candidates for stroke, heart attack, high blood pressure, kidney failure, and a host of other physical and psychological problems.

● No one living in our modern world is immune to the effects of stress. The only way to overcome stress is by minimizing your exposure to it and by learning to be unaffected by it.

● In a stress-free world, it would not be necessary to practice stress-elimination techniques. But in our contemporary world, it is essential to compensate for the extraordinary amounts of stress you are subjected to each day. Stress reduction techniques that are easy to use, effective, and make minimal demands upon your time and energy, are a necessary part of any stress relief program.

● Along with stress-elimination techniques, it is necessary to put into practice strategies that will effectively help you to minimize and overcome unavoidable environmental stresses.

● The greatest cause of psychological stress is expectation. Expectation is frustration. Whenever you expect *anything*, you are placing yourself in an emotionally vulnerable position and paving the way for tension and stress.

● Proper exercise and a balanced diet are an essential part of any stress reduction program. But an overemphasis on diet and exercise can create more stress than it eliminates. Approach modifications in your diet and exercise with moderation. It is advisable to consult your doctor before adopting the suggestions for changes in diet and exercise that are presented in this book.

● Stress begins at home. It is essential to deal with territorial stress. Each member of your living unit should have a defined space of his own. Do not violate the space of others and request that they do not violate your space.

● Love can ease or cause stress. Try to love unconditionally, without expecting anything in return. Do not expect to learn to love unconditionally overnight. Be content to make constant progress in the direction of unconditional love.

● Relaxed sleep is essential for your physical and mental well-being. When you fail to get enough sleep, your resistance to stress can become dangerously low. Implement constructive changes in your sleeping environment and in your attitudes towards sleep and sleeplessness so that you can get a good night's sleep.

● Don't work too hard at being relaxed. Try to implement those parts of the Total Relaxation Program which suit your needs. Use the program to improve the quality of your life.

But be flexible in your application of the strategies and techniques contained in the program. The choice is yours. You can lead a stress-free life or be subject to the debilitating effects of tension and stress. It is up to you to choose what you want. Choose wisely and choose now!

Some Final Thoughts

You are holding in your hands the most advanced, complete, and effective guide for overcoming worry, stress, tension, and fatigue. The Total Relaxation Program works. Thousands of people use the techniques and strategies every day. But the key element in the program is you. Unless you are willing to implement the strategies and techniques, then nothing positive will occur. You have to motivate yourself. You now have the "tools," but you must be the one to use them.

The slogan of the Total Relaxation Program is: *Total Relaxation—You Owe It to Yourself.* This must be your attitude if Total Relaxation is to work for you. In the preceding pages I have presented a variety of strategies and techniques which will, when successfully employed, help you to overcome stress. But unless you feel that you are worth expending time and energy on, you will fail to respond to this or any other relaxation program.

You are a unique and wonderful individual whose capacities, talents, and innate worth are inestimable. You can do, see, feel, and become much more than you realize. If you will only give yourself the opportunity, you can transcend all your limitations. Life does not have to be drudgery. Life can be a radiant and joyous experience if you will only believe in the promise of both yourself and life. As Henry David Thoreau aptly remarked:

> The light which puts out our eyes is darkness to us. Only the day dawns to which we are awake. There is more day to dawn. The sun is but a morning star.

TOTAL RELAXATION TECHNIQUE #12
THE RIVER OF LIFE

Imagine that you are sitting on the bank of a great river. The river is so wide that you cannot see across it. As you look into the distance, you can see nothing but a constant movement of water. The volume of water that is flowing through the river is incomprehensible. It is all the water that has ever existed or that will ever exist.

As you watch the river flow, relax and let your life flow with it. Feel that the river is taking you back through everything you have ever known. If you look deeply into the river, you will be able to see all of the people, places, and things that you have experienced in your lifetime. Watch them pass by as you sit on the bank of the river of life.

Listen to the sound of the river. You can hear its steady sound as it passes in front of you. It is the pulse of all life. Lose yourself in the sound of the river. Feel that you and the river are merging and becoming one. Allow yourself to flow along with the river of life and let it join you as it will with any elements it contains.

Flow on endlessly with the river of life. Don't try to direct your course. You are flowing on, protected by the strength and the guidance of the river. Relax and picture yourself endlessly flowing on with the river of existence . . .

When you feel you have relaxed as much as you would like, visualize that you are again sitting on the bank of the river. You have been totally relaxed by your journey and now are ready to re-enter peacefully the flow of your own life.

APPENDIX

TOTAL RELAXATION TECHNIQUE #1

THE BLUE SKY

Picture a beautiful blue sky without any clouds in it. As you picture the clear blue sky, feel that your body is growing lighter and lighter. Close your eyes and keep the image of the blue sky in your mind. There are no limits to the blue sky. It stretches endlessly in every direction, never beginning and never ending. As you visualize the blue sky, feel that your body has become so light that you have floated up into the clear blue sky. Feel that you are floating in the sky and that all tension, fatigue, worry, and problems have left you. Relax your mind and allow your breathing to seek its own level. Feel yourself floating gently in the clear blue sky which stretches endlessly in every direction, never beginning and never ending.

After several minutes have passed and you feel yourself relaxing, then picture that your entire body is merging with the blue sky. Your body is merging with the peace of the blue sky ... Your mind is merging with the tranquility of the blue sky ... Feel that you have actually become the blue sky. You no longer have a body or a mind. You have become the infinite blue sky that stretches endlessly in every direction, never beginning and never ending. Feel that you have become the perfect peace and tranquility of the blue sky. Completely let go and experience Total Relaxation.

When you feel that you have relaxed for as long as you like, then open your eyes. You will now have a new and deeper sense of peace, relaxation, and poise. This renewed energy, joy, and calm will stay with you as you resume your normal activities.

TOTAL RELAXATION TECHNIQUE #2
THE TOWER OF LIGHT

Take a deep breath and exhale slowly. As you exhale, mentally picture all tiredness, tension, and fatigue leaving you. Relax. Turn your attention to the crown of your head. Visualize that a wave of golden light is entering into you at the top of your head and passing throughout your entire body. Imagine this golden light passing from the crown of your head, through your neck, shoulders, arms, chest, stomach, lower back, and down your legs to your feet.

As you imagine the golden light passing throughout your body, feel yourself relaxing. Picture another wave of golden light entering in through the crown of your head and visualize it passing through your entire body and then leaving through the soles of your feet. Feel that wave after wave of golden light is passing through you in this way. Each wave of golden light that passes through your body removes more of your tension and helps you to enter further and deeper into a state of total relaxation.

Picture that the waves of golden light have now become a solid river of golden light which is constantly passing through you. Picture this golden light expanding beyond your body and filling up the entire room. Then visualize the golden light expanding beyond the earth ... beyond the sky ... into the infinite. Feel that the golden light is constantly passing through you and washing all of your tensions, problems, and worries beyond you, beyond the earth ... beyond the sky ... into the infinite. Continue visualizing the golden stream of light passing through you into the infinite for as long as you choose to relax.

TOTAL RELAXATION TECHNIQUE #3
THE OCEAN

Imagine a vast ocean. The ocean is filled with hundreds and thousands of waves. Feel that you are part of that ocean. Imagine that each wave in the ocean is slowly moving through you. Feel that each wave is a wave of joy. Imagine wave after wave of joy passing through your whole body. As each wave passes through your body, feel that all worries, tensions, anxieties, and problems are being washed away in the successive waves of joy. For several minutes, imagine wave after wave of joy passing through you. Feel that each wave of joy that passes through you increases the amount of joy that you now have, until you feel that you have become all joy. Nothing exists for you except limitless, boundless joy.

Now imagine that you are going beneath the surface of the ocean. The surface of the ocean is filled with many waves, but below the surface, in the depths, all is calm, silent, and serene. Imagine yourself sinking slowly into the depths of the ocean. Here there is only calmness, quiet, and tranquility. As you imagine yourself going deeper and deeper into the depths of the ocean, feel that peace is entering into you. Feel that the deeper you go into the inner ocean, the more peaceful and calm you become. Feel that there is no end to the depths of this ocean. It goes on endlessly. Imagine yourself sinking deeper and deeper into the endless ocean, feeling more peace and more tranquility filling your entire being until you have become all peace, and all tranquility.

TOTAL RELAXATION TECHNIQUE #4

THE SPHERE OF POWER

Practice this Total Relaxation exercise whenever you feel tension entering into you from outside. This exercise can be practiced while you work, talk with others, drive a car, or engage in any activity. This exercise is particularly effective when you need to stop tension, frustration, or panic immediately.

Focus your attention upon the center of your stomach, in the area of your navel. Feel that this is an area of tremendous strength. Visualize a clear sphere, a dome of energy surrounding your entire body, which is supported by your own willpower. Positive thoughts, feelings, ideas, and vibrations can pass through this sphere and reach you. But as long as you visualize this sphere of clear energy surrounding you, negative thoughts, hostilities, anger, and aggressive feelings of other persons and situations cannot enter you.

While you imagine this sphere of clear energy surrounding you, feel that you are consciously directing energy from the center of your body, in the area of your navel, throughout the sphere. Feel that the energy of your willpower can easily deflect tension-causing feelings and frustrations that are directed inside you from the outside world. You will find that with repeated practice it becomes easier and easier to visualize this sphere of energy, and that you will be able to stop the negative energy of others from entering you.

THE ROSE

Visualize a beautiful rose in the center of your chest. It is not necessary, when doing this exercise, to see a clear picture of the rose. Simply do the best you can to imagine a soft, reddish rose in the center of your chest. If other thoughts and images pass through your mind while you're performing this exercise, simply ignore them.

Imagine that the rose is completely folded up; none of the petals has unfolded. Now, as you focus your attention upon the reddish rose in the center of your chest, imagine that the first set of petals, the outer row of petals, are gradually unfolding. As they do so, imagine them growing and expanding and filling the entire area of your chest. Simultaneously feel that a wave of peace and joy is spreading throughout your entire chest area. Then imagine that a second set of rose petals is unfolding. Slowly and gently they unfold and expand, this time filling the entire area of your body. And again, feel another wave of peace and joy, even deeper than the first, starting in the center of the chest, in the center of the rose, and expanding outwards, filling your entire body with peace and joy. Now visualize a third set of petals, again starting in the center of the rose, and imagine them expanding outwards, filling up the entire room, spreading peace and joy everywhere throughout the room or area in which you are located. Then visualize a fourth set of petals opening up, this time expanding and filling the entire earth. Feel that peace and joy are spreading from the center of your chest, from the center of the rose, throughout all of the earth, and filling all of the people, all of the beings and all of the objects on this earth with peace and joy. Now visualize another set of petals opening up, this time filling the entire solar system. And simultaneously feel that you are spreading your own

TOTAL RELAXATION TECHNIQUE #6
SWIRLING LIGHT

Focus your attention upon the center of your forehead. Imagine that there is a slow but steady swirling of white light there. The white light is very soft and gentle. Visualize that this white light is slowly moving in a clockwise direction. Visualize that the swirling white light is slowly expanding. As it does, the white light begins to encompass the other portions of your body. Imagine the soft white light expanding in a circular swirling motion until your entire body has become lost in it.

Feel that the room that you are sitting in is becoming filled with the swirling white light. Visualize that the light is expanding beyond the room to encompass the building or area in which you are located. Then imagine that the white light is expanding even further to encompass all of the area for miles around you. Finally visualize the soft white light continuing to expand as it gently swirls around, until it has filled the earth, the sky, the universe, and all of infinity.

Let go. Allow yourself to merge with the slowly swirling white light. Feel that nothing else exists but this ever-present calm, peaceful white light. There is no yesterday, no tomorrow, no future or past. Your mind is calm and relaxed. All that exists is swirling white light, and you have become part of that light. Relax, continue to visualize the swirling white light, and experience peace.

TOTAL RELAXATION TECHNIQUE #7
DEEP RELAXATION

This technique is an extremely effective method of relaxing the entire body. Many people find that practicing it for fifteen to twenty minutes will give them the benefits of rest and relaxation that they would have gained from three to four hours of sleep. If you suffer from insomnia or other sleep disorders, then practicing this technique can help you make up for a great deal of lost sleep. It is also especially helpful when you are in demanding situations in which you don't have the opportunity to get enough sleep.

Lie down on your back and assume a comfortable position. Keep your palms upward and your head in a straight, but natural position. Now, fold your hands into fists and tense every muscle in your body, just for a moment. Then, quickly relax. Relax all of the muscles in your body. Again, tense every muscle, making fists with your hands, curling your toes, and slightly arching the spine. Then, abruptly relax all the muscles. Take a deep breath, then slowly exhale. Inhale again, and visualize peace entering in through the top of your head. Exhale slowly, visualizing all pain, tiredness, tension, and fatigue leaving through the soles of your feet. Again inhale, visualizing peace entering in through the crown of your head. Again slowly exhale, visualizing fatigue, anxiety, worry, and tension leaving through the soles of your feet. Now relax and breathe normally.

Beginning at the top of your head, relax every muscle in your body, and every part of your body. Begin by relaxing the scalp, then the head. Relax your forehead, your cheeks, nose, mouth, facial muscles. Allow the jaw to sag, but keep the lips closed. Relax the back of your head, relax the neck and shoulders. Then relax your chest. Feel all of your ribs relaxing. Relax your spine. Feel your spine gently touching the floor, and relax it vertebra by vertebra. Relax your stomach and lower back. Now relax your pelvis. Relax your abdomen, hips, and base of the spine. Relax your thighs, knees, calves, ankles. Relax your feet, toes, and the soles of your feet. Check over your entire body from the top of your head to the soles of your feet, looking for any signs of tension. When you find tense muscles, consciously relax them.

After you feel that you've relaxed all the muscles of your body, then turn your attention inward, to your internal organs. Your internal organs work very hard for you, both day and night, while you are awake and while you are asleep. They, too, need to relax in order to work more efficiently. Relax your lungs; allow your breathing to become easy. Relax the heart; focus your attention on your heartbeat to find that you can consciously slow down the beating of the heart, thus relaxing it. Relax your stomach muscles. Consciously relax the whole area of the stomach within the physical body. Relax the bladder and intestines.

Now relax your mind. Your mind should remain calm and alert, but totally relaxed. When thoughts pass in and out of your mind, simply ignore them. Imagine that you are a tiny bubble floating in an infinite ocean of peace and light. Now imagine that the little bubble of yourself, of your consciousness, is breaking and gently dissolving into the ocean of peace and light that stretches endlessly in every direction, never beginning and never ending. Feel that the little bubble of your consciousness now has totally dissolved and merged into the ocean of light and peace, and you have become the infinite ocean of light and peace, stretching endlessly in every direction.

Now, having completely relaxed the mind and body, simply let go and enjoy the peace of total relaxation.

TOTAL RELAXATION TECHNIQUE #8
THE WHITE BIRD

Picture yourself as a beautiful white bird. Feel that you are flying high up in a cloudless sky. Imagine that you are gently flapping your wings and flying higher and higher until the earth fades from your sight.

Now try gliding. Feel that you are floating on the air currents high above this world. Imagine yourself soaring and then swooping down. Feel the perfect freedom of unobstructed flight. You are flying alone high up in the sky. You have flown beyond all of your problems, worries, and difficulties.

Fly higher, beyond the sky into space. Fly between the stars and planets. Glide beyond all of the distant heavens until you have flown beyond time and space. Continue flying into worlds unknown.

Feel that you are flying now into other dimensions. You are passing through dimension after dimension. Each dimension is a different reality and you have glimpses of that reality as you pass through it. Feel that you are flying through hundreds of different dimensions each minute.

As you fly through each dimension, notice your bird body changing. It will assume a different shape in each dimension. Then, after flying through all of existence, return to this world. Fly high up in the sky and then swoop down to your home.

Fly back into your room and observe your body as it relaxes. Now re-enter your body. As you do, feel that you are bringing back with you a totally new perspective on existence. All of the freedom and vision you gained from your flight will stay with you now. You have experienced perfect freedom in flight. Your flying has totally relaxed and refreshed you.

TOTAL RELAXATION TECHNIQUE #9
ASSOCIATIVE RELAXATION

Lie down on your back. Take a deep breath and slowly exhale. Relax. Think of the color green for a moment. Imagine that your feet, ankles, legs, knees, and thighs are being bathed in a beautiful green light. Now relax these parts of your body. Continue relaxing them until all tension has left.

Think of the color purple. Imagine that your stomach, abdomen, lower back, and lower ribs are being filled with purple light. Now consciously relax these areas of your body until they are completely relaxed.

Visualize your chest, upper torso, back, and ribs. Feel that they are being bathed in a beautiful light-blue light. Now relax these parts of your body until all stress and tension has left them.

Feel the area of your shoulders, neck, face, and head. Imagine that they are surrounded with a beautiful golden light. Now consciously relax these parts of your body until they are completely relaxed.

After you have completed this process, then imagine that your whole body is being bathed in a glowing white light. Now relax your entire body until all signs of tension have left you.

After you have practiced this technique a number of times, you will be able to use it to relax specific sections of your body at any time. For example, if you find that your stomach is tense while you are driving or at a meeting, then imagine that it is being filled with purple light. Your muscles should relax very quickly. If you develop a headache or a tight neck, imagine that this area of your body is being bathed in golden light. If you feel a tightness around your chest, then imagine that your chest is being bathed in a light-blue light, and so on. The more you practice, the better and more quickly the technique will work. Eventually you should be able to relax any part of your body within moments of visualizing the color you associated with it.

TOTAL RELAXATION TECHNIQUE #10
THE FIELD OF LIGHT

Visualize a field that is surrounded by large trees on all sides. The field is in full bloom. Hundreds of wildflowers dot the tall green grass that is gently blowing back and forth in the wind.

The field is filled with the melodious and soothing singing of birds. You can hear several different types of bird songs all around you. The sky above the field is a cloudless cerulean blue. The breeze is slight and the temperature is comfortable.

Picture yourself in the middle of the field. You are lying on your back gazing up at the sky. All around you is life. You are basking in the sunlight, looking into the cool blue sky.

As you stare into the sky, feel transported. The boundaries of your awareness extend themselves and you merge with the field. Feel that you are one with all the life of the field. You exist in each of the beautifully colored flowers that are swaying gently in the breeze. You are part of the tall green grass. You are the melodious songs of the birds. You are all of the life that exists in the field and you are able to feel and sense all of the life processes that are taking place there.

The sky is above you. It stretches on into the beyond. Your awareness expands and you become part of the sky. Then you find yourself back in the field.

The field is filled with light. Everything seems to glow and radiate. The sunlight reflects off each flower and blade of grass and sparkles in thousands of colors. Each one of these colors is a part of what you are. You merge with them and become them.

All of the colors stem from one white light. You go back to your own source and become that light. Nothing exists but that white light. All things come forth from it and eventually return to it. For as long as you choose to relax, feel that you are the white shining light that underlies all of existence. When you feel that you have relaxed for as long as you would like, imagine yourself coming back into the field. For a moment, pause and look around the field. Fix in your mind what everything looks like. This field of light is always waiting for you whenever you need to come to it. Remember it and come back to it whenever you need to. Then open your eyes and return, refreshed and relaxed from your sojourn in the field of light.

TOTAL RELAXATION TECHNIQUE #11
THE CLOUDS

Visualize that you are sitting on top of a very high mountain. The sky above you is filled with puffy white clouds. The banks of white clouds are gently drifting over your head. As you watch them you find yourself feeling very relaxed.

Feel that your body is becoming very light. You are so light that you are starting to float. Your body is rising above the mountain top and is floating up into the clouds. You are surrounded by beautiful white puffy clouds on all sides.

Feel that you are floating with the clouds. As you drift with the clouds you are losing track of time. Today, yesterday, and tomorrow have all merged together. All that exists for you is timeless floating high above the earth.

As you float in the sky you are conscious that you are passing over oceans, deserts, forests, and cities. You are above and beyond them all as you are blown forward by the winds of existence. Continue visualizing yourself floating with the clouds for as long as you like. Simply drift with the white clouds and relax ...

When you are totally relaxed, picture that you are again among the mountains. Visualize the mountain you were originally sitting on. Feel that your body is growing heavier and that you are drifting back down to the mountain top. Imagine yourself sitting on top of the mountain, completely refreshed and relaxed after your journey with the clouds.

TOTAL RELAXATION TECHNIQUE #12

THE RIVER OF LIFE

Imagine that you are sitting on the bank of a great river. The river is so wide that you cannot see across it. As you look into the distance, you can see nothing but a constant movement of water. The volume of water that is flowing through the river is incomprehensible. It is all the water that has ever existed or that will ever exist.

As you watch the river flow, relax and let your life flow with it. Feel that the river is taking you back through everything you have ever known. If you look deeply into the river, you will be able to see all of the people, places, and things that you have experienced in your lifetime. Watch them pass by as you sit on the bank of the river of life.

Listen to the sound of the river. You can hear its steady sound as it passes in front of you. It is the pulse of all life. Lose yourself in the sound of the river. Feel that you and the river are merging and becoming one. Allow yourself to flow along with the river of life and let it join you as it will with any elements it contains.

Flow on endlessly with the river of life. Don't try to direct your course. You are flowing on, protected by the strength and the guidance of the river. Relax and picture yourself endlessly flowing on with the river of existence ...

When you feel you have relaxed as much as you would like, visualize that you are again sitting on the bank of the river. You have been totally relaxed by your journey and now are ready to re-enter peacefully the flow of your own life.

Bibliography

BENSON, HERBERT, M.D., and KLIPPER, MIRIAM Z. *The Relaxation Response.* New York: Avon Books, 1976.

FRIEDMAN, MEYER, M.D., and ROSENMAN, RAY H., M.D. *Type A Behavior and Your Heart.* New York: Fawcett, 1978.

SELYE, HANS, M.D. *Stress Without Distress.* New York: New American Library, 1975.

SRI CHINMOY. *Meditation: Man Perfection in God Satisfaction.* Published privately by Agni Press, 84-47 Parsons Blvd., Jamaica, New York 11432, 1978. This is the most comprehensive book available on the subject of meditation.

TOFFLER, ALVIN. *Future Shock.* New York: Bantam, 1971.

WEEKS, CLAIRE, M.D. *Hope and Help for Your Nerves.* New York: Bantam, 1978.

WHITE, JOHN, and FADIMAN, JAMES (eds.). *Relax: How You Can Feel Better, Reduce Stress and Overcome Tension.* New York: Dell, 1976.

Index

Printed in the United States
By Bookmasters